Faith Out Loud

A Cumberland Presbyterian
YOUTH RESOURCE
Volume 3, Quarter 3

Discipleship Ministry Team
Ministry Council
Cumberland Presbyterian Church

February 2014

8207 Traditional Place
Cordova (Memphis), Tennessee 38016

©2014 Discipleship Ministry Team

All Rights Reserved. No part of this book may be reproduced or transmitted in any form or by any means, electronic or mechanical, including photocopying, recording, or by any information storage or retrieval system, without permission in writing from the publisher with the single exception that purchase of this curriculum grants the purchaser the right to copy and distribute student handouts within each lesson for use in their local church. For information address Discipleship Ministry Team, Cumberland Presbyterian Center, 8207 Traditional Place, Cordova (Memphis), Tennessee, 38016-7414.

The Discipleship Ministry Team of the Ministry Council of the Cumberland Presbyterian Church is the successor organization to the Board of Christian Education of the Cumberland Presbyterian Church.

Funded, in part, by your contributions to Our United Outreach.

First Edition 2014

Published by The Discipleship Ministry Team, CPC
Memphis, Tennessee

ISBN-13: 978-0615965017
ISBN-10: 0615965016

We want to hear from you.
Please send your comments about this curriculum to
the Discipleship Ministry Team at faithoutloud@cumberland.org

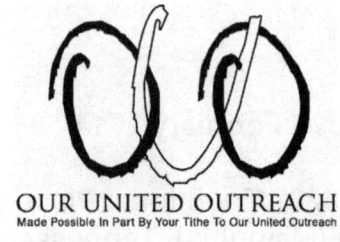

OUR UNITED OUTREACH
Made Possible In Part By Your Tithe To Our United Outreach

Table of Contents

Curriculum Users Guide. v

Lesson 1: Father, Forgive Them. 1

Lesson 2: Let's Cast Lots. 9

Lesson 3: Ha!. 21

Lesson 4: Here is Your Son. Here is Your Mother.. 31

Lesson 5: He Can't Save Himself. 45

Lesson 6: I'm Thirsty. 59

Lesson 7: Crucifixion. 69

Lesson 8: Wait, Let's See. 81

Lesson 9: Remember Me. 89

Lesson 10: Do Not Write. 103

Lesson 11: It is Finished. 111

Lesson 12: Into Your Hands, I Commit My Spirit 121

Lesson 13: Truly this was the Son of God. 135

Welcome to the Faith Out Loud curriculum!

It is our prayer that these lessons both encourage you and equip you as a youth leader—we're so grateful for what you do in the lives of students!

Blessings to you and your ministry!

Below are explanations of the components found in each lesson and tips for using this curriculum.

Lesson Title: Each lesson has a catchy title. Use these titles as teasers to get your students excited about upcoming gatherings.

Scripture: Each lesson has a key scripture reference. Spend some time studying and praying through each week's passage as you prepare to teach.

Theme: The theme statement gives you a quick snapshot into the main point of the lesson.

Leader Prep: This section is usually divided into two parts: Resource List and Leader Prep. Resource List give you a quick list of all the stuff you need to gather for each week. Leader Prep give detailed instructions on the advance work that needs to be done for that week's activities. Do NOT wait until the night before you teach to review this section.

The Lesson: Once you move into the teaching time, you'll see these recurring elements:

- ✓ **Get Started:** These activities are designed to draw students into the material and set up the theme for the lesson.

- ✓ **Discussion Questions:** Usually a group of open-ended questions, these moments in the lesson are strategically placed to encourage your students to both think about and respond to the topic at hand.

- ✓ **Say:** Placed in italics, these sections can be read verbatim to your students to help them fully understand the implications of the topic or theme. You'll discover you'll get the best response when you are thoroughly familiar with these sections and can deliver the same information in your own words instead of just reading the info to the students.

- ✓ **Leader Tips:** You'll find sections of side notes throughout each lesson. These are notes just for you, the leader. These notes offer you everything from instructions on how to facilitate the activities to background information on the subject to tips for making your lesson run smoothly.

- ✓ **Listen Up:** This section highlights a key scripture passage that should be read aloud. Encourage student to do these readings as often as possible.

- ✓ **Now What:** This section helps your students respond to the lesson. This will drive the lesson home and get your students thinking about the lesson in terms outside of the classroom walls.

- ✓ **Live It:** This is simply just the closing of each lesson, designed to help you conclude your time with your students well and offer them something to think about in the week ahead. Most weeks have handouts to pass along to your students during this time. You may find it helpful to encourage your students to get a folder to keep these handouts together so they can easily refer to them during the week.

- ✓ **Handouts:** At the end of some lessons, you'll find a reproducible page. Your purchase of this curriculum grants you the right to print and distribute copies to everyone in your group.

- ✓ **Just in Case/Digging Deeper:** These provide opportunities to continue the lesson and enable further learning.

Father, Forgive them
by Christopher Anderson

Scripture: Luke 23:34

Theme: Jesus taught us to forgive not just those we care about, but our enemies, too. How do we reconcile a broken world through the love of Jesus?

Resource List

- Music for prayer and contemplation,
- Music player (laptop, iPod, MP3 player, CD player, speakers, etc.)
- Video capability (laptop, projector, DVD player, speakers, etc.)
- Video- "Wanted: God's Character"
- Construction paper
- Copy paper (8 ½ x 11)
- Scissors
- Colored pens or pencils
- Copies of the NRSV Bible

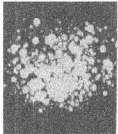

Leader Prep

- Locate the video, "Wanted: God's Character" on YouTube - http://www.youtube.com/watch?v=f7Vqi6nMAWA
- Spend time in prayer and meditation before preparing and teaching the lesson.

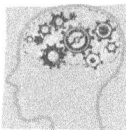

Leader Insight

Connecting to Your Students
Many youth of the millennial generation struggle to balance a virtual world with the "real" world. Staying plugged in by constantly texting on a smartphone, making 15 second videos on Vine, posting on Facebook or Instagram, or sending a tweet on Twitter suggest that youth today are seeking to connect with others in any way possible. It's important to be aware of the latest gadgets in order to build rapport with teenagers, but the common fundamental theme is that youth are starving to be in community.

Wanting to be accepted brings positive and negative results, regardless of age. However, for youth, perhaps because of their lack of experience, the negative results can seem like they outweigh the positive. It's important to listen and be

Notes:

present when interacting with a youth group. Kids are not easily fooled, and they pay attention to what adults think and feel about them. It is essential to set up an environment that fosters love and acceptance so each student will feel the freedom to be autonomous within the group. This is how God reveals gifts from the Holy Spirit.

This lesson will gradually direct your students to visualize Jesus forgiving those who were crucifying him on the cross. What does this say to youth in today's culture when the common response to harm done is revenge? How does one forgive a bully or someone who speaks badly about them behind their back?

Explaining the Bible
The Gospel according to Luke was a well-written, historical account of the life of Jesus Christ. The stories of the Good Samaritan and the Prodigal Son are only found in this gospel. Luke's account also has special emphasis on prayer, activities of the Holy Spirit, activities of women, and joyfulness. Jesus is presented as the Son of God, but special attention is paid to the humanity of Jesus and his compassion for the weak, the poor, the suffering, and the outcast. Therefore, it's not surprising to witness Jesus on the cross asking the Father to forgive the ones who were crucifying him.

It is common practice to compartmentalize the theological message of Jesus Christ, dissecting each word or sentence for further understanding. There is nothing wrong with wanting to understand the the theological nuances of the gospel of Jesus. However, one must realize that the gospel, or "good news," of Jesus was always meant to be lived out in a very practical way.

A practical theology is one that can be applied to everyday living. In the Gospel according to John, he talks about the "Word" becoming flesh. What does that mystery actually mean? Could he possibly be suggesting that Jesus was fulfilling the prophecies of the Old Testament, or is he saying that Jesus was the living manifestation of God? How does the Word of God become flesh in your life? How do you as a teacher and a Christian practice the teachings of Jesus in your own life?

Theological Underpinnings
Whether Jesus was referring to the Roman soldiers or the Jewish leaders as the groups who were killing him, the message is very clear: "Father, forgive them; for they do not know

what they are doing." The practical theological message is to forgive your enemies even when they hurt you the most. The kingdom of God will reign on earth through Jesus Christ not by war or bloodshed, but through love.

Those who heard Jesus' words were more than likely shocked. This man, hanging from a cross, forgave them. Unconditionally. What does unconditional forgiveness look like? In this lesson, we will explore Luke 23:24, in light of Jesus' suffering and the forgiveness he offered while he agonized on the cross.

In the video, "Wanted: God's Character," we will view and discuss one example of unconditional forgiveness.

The lesson will conclude with options for activities that focus on displaying forgiveness and acting out the story found in the Luke 23:34 scripture passage.

Finally, you will finish with a prayer thanking God for his word and instructions to love, pray, and forgive everybody.

Applying the Lesson to Your Own Life
When have you been forgiven?

When have you asked for forgiveness and not received it?

Forgiveness is essential in relationships. Forgiveness is also difficult. True forgiveness is unconditional and not predicated on any act or request from the offender. That's the kind of forgiveness God offers us; and the kind of forgiveness Jesus gave in this passage.

Watch the video for this lesson before you watch it with your group. What does the video say to you?

You are on a journey together in pursuit of eternal truths in the body of Christ. Anticipate that the Holy Spirit will speak to you as the leader and teacher while preparing and applying this lesson to your life. However, as the leader, facilitate an environment that permits each student to hear the Spirit as it speaks to him or her. As James says, be quick to listen and slow to speak.

Notes:

Notes:

The Lesson

Get Started (10 min.)

Prior to the beginning of class, dim the lights in the room. Candlelight is appropriate, if desired. Have instrumental music playing.

As students enter the room, invite them to sit in a circle on the floor or in chairs and to prepare their mind, body, and spirit for meditation and contemplation. Pass out a pen and paper to each member.

Read Luke 23:34.

Allow 5 minutes of contemplative music to help the group focus. Instruct them to slow their breathing with the sound of the music as they imagine Jesus on the cross. After 5 minutes is over, end in a prayer, and ask God to help you remain present throughout the lesson.

Take 5-7 minutes and go around the circle asking each participant what image they saw, or what they focused on, concerning Jesus praying for others as he suffered on the cross. It can be one word, a phrase, a sentence, a color etc. Have each student write down what they saw, and ask them to share with the group. Students could also

Listen Up (25 min.)

Watch the YouTube video, "Wanted: God's Character."

Divide into small groups or answer these as a total group. (This lesson will focus on an intentional dialogue with a solid discussion about the forgiveness of Jesus and how Christians are to imitate this forgiveness in their lives.)

Discussion Questions:
- Why is the man in the video visibly upset at the beginning? What did he lose?

- When Bill walked up to the church and saw the help wanted sign, he seemed happy. After the pastor gave him the job as the gardener, how do you think Bill felt?

- When the three kids approached Bill in the garden outside the church, what did he offer the boys? What did the boys do when Bill offered them kindness? (Bill offered them water to drink. What did Jesus say about living water?)

- Did Bill try and stop the boys from taking his possessions? How do you feel Jesus would have handled the situation?

- What did Bill greet the boys with when they returned? Why do you think Bill approached his position the same way?

- When Jeff returned with all of Bill's belongings, how did Bill react? Do you feel that Bill applied a Luke 23:34 heart during his interaction with the boys? (Bill was actually surprised and thanked him over and over. Bill was consistent with love for his enemies.)

- Bill tells Jeff that a long time ago Jesus taught people to love their enemies, unlike the "eye for an eye" attitude of the old Jewish faith. What was Jesus doing on the cross when he recited, "Father, forgive them; for they do not know what they are doing."? How hard would it be to forgive the very people who were killing you?

- When the scene fades with Bill disappearing, what do you see on the door and why? Who takes Bill's place as the gardener? Do you think Bill gave Jeff hope before he died? Do you believe that Jeff knew what he was doing when he persecuted Bill? Do you think the Roman soldiers and the Jewish leaders knew they were crucifying the Messiah?

- When Jeff approaches the pastor to share he was leaving his gardening position, what does he tell the pastor? Who does Jeff say he and his wife are naming the baby after? Do you feel that Bill's actions of forgive-

Notes:

Notes:

ness changed Jeff's life? Can you show your family and friends this kind of love?

- Do you remember the quote by Dr. Martin Luther King Jr. at the beginning of the video? In case you missed it…"Love is the only force capable of transforming an enemy into a friend." Jesus was praying for his enemies up to his last breath. Are you praying for your enemies? How can you implement this into your everyday life?

Now What? (15 min.)

Option #1

Have the group divide into pairs and each participant take some construction paper or white copy paper to draw on. Cut the paper length-wise to make two pieces. In reference to the scripture lesson for today, Luke 23:34 – "Father, forgive them; for they do not know what they are doing," and the video "Wanted: Gods Character," have each pair of participants work together to make two or more bumper stickers demonstrating the reconciliation a broken world through the Love of Jesus. They can design these anyway they wish with words, phrases, or art.

After they are finished, have each group share what they have designed with each other.

Option #2

Divide up the roles in the video, "Wanted: Gods Character," and have each participant recreate the video. After they are finished, ask each actor how it felt to play his or her chosen role.

Discussion Questions:
- What did you feel?
- How did it feel to be disconnected or connected?
- Did you get a glimpse into the life of another person?
- How do you feel about reconciliation with God after watching and recreating the video?

Option #3
Write your own short script that displays unconditional forgiveness. Use the story of, "Wanted: God's Character" for inspiration. This doesn't need to be a full script but a storyline that can be improvised. Once a storyline is decided upon, assign roles and act out the story.

Discuss how this is an example of unconditional forgiveness as found in Luke 23:34.

Live It (5 min.)

Have the group create a circle. Ask someone to start off the prayer thanking God for his word and instructions to love, pray, and forgive our enemies. Ask each person to say one word in the circle that demonstrates the love of Jesus. Finally, have the last person close in prayer asking God to help each one to "Live it".

Resources used: chemistry.about.com, John by Gerard Sloyan, mayoclinic.com, "Miracles" in God in the Dock by C.S. Lewis, wikihow.com

© 2014 Discipleship Ministry Team of the Ministry Council of the Cumberland Presbyterian Church. All Rights Reserved.

Notes:

Let's Cast Lots
by Andy McClung

Scripture: John 19:23-25

Theme: Following Christ means taking chances.

Resource List

- A quarter or other coin for each student
- $10 per student or other amount
- A dozen or so small treats (candy, pen, gum, etc.)
- (Optional) Song, "The Gambler"
- The ugliest shirt you can find
- Copy of "Taking a Gamble for God Journal" page for each student

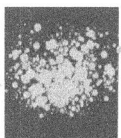

Leader Prep

- Well before class, check with the church session, and request that a certain amount of money from the appropriate line item in the church budget be used to obtain a certain amount of cash for each student in your class. Bring this cash to class. At least $10 (or other amount) per student should be enough.
- Have the song, "The Gambler" cued. Versions by Johnny Cash, Kenny Rogers, Uncle Kracker, or Blake Shelton are appropriate.

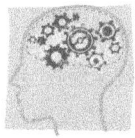

Leader Insight

Connecting to Your Students
In North America today, teens live in a gambling culture. If your state has a lottery, they see billboards proclaiming the current jackpot. They're exposed to TV and radio ads for casinos. They can watch hours of poker on ESPN. Stores and restaurants encourage them to take online surveys for a chance to win gift cards. The arcade games they play aren't about getting the high score, but rather about winning tickets to redeem for prizes. They see community groups and churches hold raffles. They watch movies and TV shows that glamorize gambling. They play video games that involve

Notes:

gambling. Their local news programs and radio stations run "first caller" contests.

Gambling is normal to them. Adults who rail against it may be dismissed as out of touch. This lesson doesn't denounce monetary gambling outright, but instead emphasizes good ways to takes chances— to risk something for Christ's sake.

Explaining the Bible
All four of the gospels mention the Roman soldiers casting lots to divide Jesus' clothing (Matthew 27:35, Mark 15:24, Luke 23:34, John 19:23-25), which may have been a perk of working crucifixion duty. Only John, however, records what the soldiers said and mentions the garment with no seams.

Why did the soldiers, if they wanted the robe, even consider cutting it up and therefore ruining it? In that time and place, there were no stores full of ready-made clothes to buy. Only the very rich owned more than one or two sets of clothes. Any piece of spun and woven fabric already had a lot of work put into it, so it had value. It could easily be sold or traded for someone to patch up another garment.

What does it mean that the robe was seamless and woven in one piece from the top? Most clothing has seams because it's easier to cut two-dimensional shapes from fabric and then sew them together. But Jesus' robe had been woven on a special loom that made it a three-dimensional, one-piece garment that didn't have different pieces of fabric sewn together. Thus it had no seams, like a sweater knitted the hard way. This was a rare and expensive article of clothing, which was why the soldiers didn't want to tear it up.

John may have been so specific about this garment so his readers would draw a connection between it being woven from the top down and what Jesus said to Nicodemus in John 3:3, a person must be born from above (the top down) to see the Kingdom of God.

Where did Jesus get a robe that was so nice? His parents were poor. He was a poor, wandering rabbi who apparently relied on the kindness of others for the basic necessities of life. So, we can only assume that someone gave him the robe as a gift. Perhaps it was made especially for him, or perhaps someone who made such robes for a living gave one to Jesus as a gift. Luke 8:1-3 says that a handful of women helped support Jesus' ministry; perhaps the gift came from one of the women named there.

Was this an undergarment or an outer garment? Different translations of the Bible call Jesus' special garment different things: a tunic, shirt, coat, robe, or undergarment. So it's not perfectly clear if this was an undergarment or an outer garment, but the best guess is probably an undergarment. Since we know that the victims of crucifixion were naked as they were flogged as well as when they hung on their crosses, it's reasonable to assume that the soldiers threw the victims' undergarments back on them for the walk through the city. It's also reasonable to assume that a seamless garment would be most beneficial as an undergarment, as there would be no seams to rub against the skin. Of course, one could also argue that the nicest garment would be worn on the outside where it could be seen and admired.

What does it mean to cast lots? Some Christians have used this scene from the gospels to condemn gambling, saying that the soldiers threw dice to gamble over Jesus' clothes. Although casting lots was a kind of gambling, it had little to do with dice games as we know them. We don't know exactly what was involved in casting lots, but it was probably more like flipping a coin; drawing straws; pulling names out of hat; or even playing "one potato, two potato;" or "eeny, meeny, miny, mo" than it was like rolling dice. The biblical references to casting lots seem to indicate it was more of a way to divide up something than a game someone wins and someone loses. Followers of God also used it as a means of discerning God's will in situations. In Leviticus 16, the first high priest Aaron cast lots to determine certain things. In Numbers, lots were cast to determine which tribes got what real estate in the Promised Land. In Jonah 1, the sailors cast lots to see whose fault the storm was. In Luke 1, we see that the Temple priests sometimes cast lots to determine which of them did certain things. In Acts 1, the apostles cast lots to find Judas Iscariot's replacement.

In Psalm 22, which is a prayer asking God for deliverance from suffering and hostility, the psalmist (probably David) writes in verse 18, "they divide my clothes among themselves, and for my clothing they cast lots" (NRSV). These words are prophetic because they not only expressed the writer's feelings and fears at the time, they also point to what happened to Jesus on the cross centuries later. It's no wonder Jesus had this psalm in mind as he hung upon the cross and even spoke the opening line.

Notes:

Notes:

Theological Underpinnings

Casting lots is a form of trying to tell the future or gain divine guidance. Historically, pagan shamans cast lots—stones, sticks, bones—to "reveal the will of the gods," which usually just happened to be whatever the shaman wanted to happen. In other words, this was bogus. Without God behind it, casting lots is as reasonable as reading tea leaves or believing that how the planets and stars happened to be arranged at one's birth dictates his or her personality and fate.

However, God apparently approved (for a time) something similar to the casting of lots. The Urim and Thummin were items kept in a pouch, called an ephod, on the breastplate of the high priest's garb (Exodus 28:30, Leviticus 8:8). These were a God-given way to discern between two or more choices or to receive a 'yes' or 'no' answer from God. The Urim and Thummin were either shaken out of the ephod or blindly drawn. They may have been two flat stones with "curse" and "perfect" written in Hebrew on either side. Two "curses" meant God said "No." Two "perfects" meant God said "Yes." A mixed pair meant "no reply."

This was never seen as a human forcing God to "speak" but rather a way to determine God's will. The use of Urim and Thummin was dropped when God started speaking through prophets. Christians never picked up the practice because, as Jesus promised, after his resurrection and ascension, the Holy Spirit came to dwell within and among believers. It is now through the Holy Spirit that we discern God's will. Cumberland Presbyterians believe God reveals his will through scripture, nature, events of history, the life of Jesus Christ, and the work of the Holy Spirit (Confession of Faith 1.08, 4.01).

While God doesn't use lot casting, God is not opposed to taking risks. Giving humankind the free will to choose whether or not to respond to God's love is a risk. Suffering and dying for the redemption of the world was a risk because not everyone will accept that gift. Calling sinful humans to be the Body of Christ in the world is a risk because we don't always listen for God's will; and even when we do, we don't always follow it.

Applying the Lesson to Your Own Life

Have you ever wished you had a Urim and Thummin set—just toss those stones to know what God wanted? Why is it so hard sometimes to determine God's will?

Do you gamble for money: lottery tickets, casinos, sweep

stakes, or buy raffle tickets for prizes? What do you believe God thinks about this?

Do you gamble in other ways: driving over the speed limit, taking poor care of your body, not having insurance? What do you believe God thinks about this?

Do you gamble/take chances for Christ's sake: showing love to people you'd rather avoid, offering hospitality to strangers, doing ministry in ways you aren't trained for, undergoing training to do more ministry, giving more than your tithe? Does your church take risks for Christ's sake?

What are the risks of always playing it safe, both personally and as a congregation?

The Lesson

 ## Get Started (10 min.)

Optional: Have the song "The Gambler" playing as students gather. This is to set the mood and introduce the topic.

As students enter the classroom, give each of them a coin. All coins should be of the same value. An alternative to this is to contact all of your regular students during the week and instruct them each to bring a quarter to class; then you would only need to bring a few coins for sporadic attendees, unexpected visitors, and forgetful students.

To begin the lesson, play a game that works the same way casting lots may have worked. Announce that heads is "in" and tails is "out." Have everybody flip their coins at the same time and in the same way (i.e. flip and catch; or flip, catch, and turn over; or flip and let land on the floor). All players whose coins show tails are out. They sit down. All players whose coins show heads are still in; they retrieve their coins

Notes:

Notes:

and play again.

In this way, keep going until you eliminate all but one player. This player is the person who receives the ugly shirt. It doesn't matter if the shirt is gender specific or not.

If you have a small group the game will go quickly. If the coins land just right, the game will go quickly. If the game goes too quickly, start a new game, with the last player remaining being the recipient of one of the small treats you brought. Try making up other, non-material prizes (read the scripture in today's lesson, sit in the front seat on the next group outing, etc.)

Listen Up (20 min.)

Indicate the ugly shirt and ask the class:
- How much would you pay for a shirt/blouse like that?

Discussion Questions:
- How much would you pay for a shirt/blouse that you liked and wanted?
- How much would you pay for a shirt/blouse that had been worn by somebody else?
- What if that "somebody else" was a celebrity? Then how much would you pay?

Allow responses and discussion. Draw out further responses with questions such as:
- Whose already-worn shirt would you want to buy?
- Would you want it to be washed before you got it or not?

Explain that you will now play a game. You are going to name a used article of clothing, once worn by a celebrity, which somebody really bought. The students' task is to come closest to naming the actual purchase price.

Ham it up, like a bad game show host. Randomly choose two students to be the first two contestants. Have them stand in front of the class.

The rules: you will name an item and the contestants each get one guess. Whichever guess is closest wins. Contestants may call out their guesses at the same time. The winning contestant stays; the other is replaced by another student.

Here are the items and their actual selling prices, in no particular order.

> Scarlet Johansson's underwear: $100
> Michael Jackson's sequin glove: $350,000
> Troy Polamalu's football jersey: $600
> Dean Martin's tuxedo pants: $545
> Jennifer Aniston's bra: $65
> Melissa Hunter's overall shorts: $45
> Kim Kardashian's dress: $3,500
> Alex Rodriguez's baseball jersey: $8,050
> Michael Jordan basketball jersey: $5,000

Close the game by congratulating the winners.

Discussion Questions:
- Why do you think people are willing to pay so much money for clothes worn by somebody famous?
- What if somebody had an article of clothing that belonged to Jesus? How much do you think that would be worth?

Have someone read aloud John 19:23-25.

Using the background information, explain what casting lots was and what it wasn't.

Say: *You all are too young to gamble in a casino or to gamble by buying lottery tickets, but you do take risks in other ways. So besides gambling for money, how do you gamble? In other words, what do you do that might bring you something good or might cause you to lose something?*

Allow discussion. If your students need prompting, suggest:
- Speeding may get you there quicker, but you risk getting a ticket or having an accident.
- Playing sports is fun, good exercise, and might boost popularity, but you also risk injury.
- Smoking makes you feel cool and grown up but you risk addiction, cancer, emphysema, and turning off prospective boyfriends/girlfriends.

After a bit of discussion, say that you will name some risky be-

Notes:

Notes:

havior, and the class is to determine if that would be a good bet/risk (more likely to bring good consequences) or a bad bet/risk (more likely to bring negative consequences).

Actually, you're going to have more than that in mind. For each behavior mentioned, ask:
1. Is this a good bet or bad bet (i.e. more likely to bring a positive or negative consequence)
2. What are some possible good consequences?
3. What are some possible bad consequences?
4. Are the possible good consequences worth risking the possible bad consequences?

Allow some debate or discussion with each behavior mentioned. Have less discussion at first and more as you work down the list.
1. Singing karaoke in public
2. Asking out a boy/girl whom you like
3. Not studying for a test
4. Dancing in public
5. Taking an difficult elective class at school
6. Reporting a teacher's misbehavior
7. Lying to your parents
8. Standing up to a bully
9. Shoplifting something small and inexpensive
10. Riding with a driver who's been drinking
11. Sneaking into a construction site after dark
12. Vandalizing the school
13. Being in a relationship (having a steady boyfriend/girlfriend)
14. Being alone with your boyfriend/girlfriend… at his/her house… with his/her parents out of town
15. Volunteering to do some chores for an elderly neighbor
16. Giving money to a beggar
17. Giving a meal to a beggar
18. Telling a stranger about Jesus
19. Telling a friend about Jesus
20. Being nice to the least popular kid at school
21. Becoming friends with the least popular kid at school
22. Doing what you believe God wants you to do instead of what you want to do, or what your parents want you to do, or what your friends expect you to do

Now What? (15 min.)

Announce that this lesson has some homework involved. There are two different assignments; a flip of the coin will determine who gets which assignment.

Have students stand and get out their coins again. Have everyone flip their coins at the same time and in the same way. Then separate the class: those who got "heads" on one side of the room and those who got "tails" on the other. If you have a small class or have plenty of time, students could do this coin toss individually and watch each "team" slowly form. Announce that the assignment is to do a bit of gambling this week. Each student is expected to find some way to take a risk for Christ's sake.

Those who got "heads" are to gamble one hour of their week doing something for someone else in the name of Jesus. It could be anything that they believe would please God. If you think it's necessary, make some suggestions: visit someone in a nursing home, volunteer to mow an elderly neighbor's grass, babysit for free, spend time with the kid at school whom everyone makes fun of.

Those who got "tails" are to gamble $10 (or whatever amount you chose) doing something for someone else in the name of Jesus. Give out the money and explain that they can do anything with the money they think would please God. If you think it's necessary, make some suggestions: buy a meal for a panhandler, leave a bigger than normal tip at a restaurant along with a note that says "Jesus love you," buy a stranger a couple gallons of gas, take out a non-Christian friend for a cheeseburger and talk to him or her about Jesus, send the money to Heifer International and challenge friends and family to join you. Depending on your students' financial situations, you might challenge your students to use their own money to double the amount you give them before using it.

Give each student a, "Taking a Gamble for God Journal" page. Encourage them to start using it today, and take their gamble before class next week.

Notes:

DIGGING DEEPER

There has been great interest over the centuries in the physical objects associated with Jesus, the original disciples, and other saints—everything from articles of clothing to bits of their bodies. These objects are called relics. The relics with a direct connection to Jesus, of course, were the most sought after, especially those related to his crucifixion and resurrection. Most people have heard of the Shroud of Turin that is supposedly the burial cloth of Jesus on which his image was somehow imprinted. But that's not the half of it. In the Middle Ages, cathedrals were built around relics. People would undertake long and difficult pilgrimages just to see one. There are legends about the spear which was used to pierce Jesus' side; it is said to grant whoever possesses it long life and make him invincible in battle. Both the nails and pieces of the cross are said to bring healing. The crown of thorns was supposedly divided among several monarchs. Everything from Jesus' sandals to the post he was tied to during the flogging have all supposedly been preserved and are on display somewhere. There are several places that claim to have Jesus' seamless robe, or portions of it. Some actually have the garments on display. A 1942 novel The Robe, and its 1952 movie adaptation by the same name, follows the life of the soldier who won the robe through casting lots. (SPOILER ALERT: He ends up becoming a Christian.)

Live It (5 min.)

Close this lesson with this, or a similar, prayer: Thank you, God, for taking a chance on us by becoming human and suffering on the cross. Help us to make good choices in the risks we take. Give us wisdom and courage to take good gambles for you this week. May what we each choose to do with this money or that one hour be pleasing to you and helpful to someone.

Resources used: ebay.com, foxnews.com, reuters.com, Seven Words of Men Around the Cross, by Paul Moore, The New Bible Dictionary

© 2014 Discipleship Ministry Team of the Ministry Council of the Cumberland Presbyterian Church. All Rights Reserved.

TAKING A GAMBLE FOR GOD JOURNAL

I, _____ am going to spend (circle one) **one hour** / $_____ this week doing something in the name of Christ. I understand that this is taking a risk.

IDEA #1:
- Is this a good bet or bad bet?
- Is this something that would please God?
- What are some possible good consequences?
- What are some possible bad consequences?
- Are the possible good consequences worth the risk of the possible bad consequences?

ACCEPT / REJECT

IDEA #2:
- Is this a good bet or bad bet?
- Is this something that would please God?
- What are some possible good consequences?
- What are some possible bad consequences?
- Are the possible good consequences worth the risk of the possible bad consequences?

ACCEPT / REJECT

IDEA #3:
- Is this a good bet or bad bet?
- Is this something that would please God?
- What are some possible good consequences?
- What are some possible bad consequences?
- Are the possible good consequences worth the risk of the possible bad consequences?

ACCEPT / REJECT

Resources to get:

People to contact:

Date and time to do it:

Reflections on how it went:

Ha!
by Andy McClung

Scripture: Mark 15:29-30

Theme: How do we respond to people who either assume Christianity is a waste of time or who openly ridicule our faith?

Resource List

- Lots of art supplies, as varied as possible
- Various translations of the Bible
- Marker board or newsprint, markers

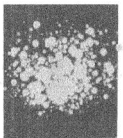

Leader Prep

- Gather several Bibles of different translations, or print out Mark 15:29-30 from several different translations
- Before class gather as wide a variety of art supplies as you can:
  - Paper of different sizes, colors, and textures
  - Pencils, crayons, markers, colored pencils, pens
  - Bits of fabric and string
  - Popsicle/craft sticks
  - Scissors, glue, and various kinds of tape
  - Maybe even sheets of sandpaper
  - Anything and everything.

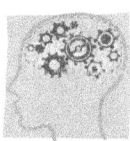

Leader Insight

Connecting to Your Students
Your students probably have peers who have never been inside a church building, who have never heard a sermon or Bible lesson, who have never picked up a Bible, whose only knowledge of Christianity is what they glean from info-tainment news shows and twitter feeds. Your students have also had a lot more exposure to other faiths than previous generations. They've witnessed Christian beliefs repeatedly attacked, both subtly and overtly. They've probably met persons both apathetic and hostile toward Christianity. The funny thing is, while it may seem to older generations like these things are

Notes:

new, except for the different technology used, Christians and Christianity have been dealing with this stuff since the early church began.

In this lesson, your task is to help your students understand that not everyone sees Christianity as they do, and encourage them to seek effective ways of sharing Christ with such people.

Explaining the Bible

From what we know about Roman executions, it's likely that during Jesus' six hours on the cross a lot of people walked by him as he hung there, many of them ridiculed him as they passed, and some folks went out of their way to approach Jesus and ridicule him. Mark 15:29-30 shows us some of this. These people were just plain, ordinary, First Century Jewish folks. They were poor; not working for more than a day or two meant running out of money for food, and they owned only one outer garment and two lightweight undergarments. As had many generations before them, they'd heard all their lives how the Messiah would one day come and save their nation from its worst enemy. This promise was in the scriptures they quoted daily, in the songs they sang, and in the prayers they said.

They thought their worst enemy was the Roman Empire that had conquered and was occupying their homeland. As a people, they had forgotten had forgotten that, like all humans, sin and death were their worst enemies. They had interpreted God's promise of a savior to mean a Messiah swooping down in a blaze of glory and destroying the Romans in some kind of grand political or military action, and showing the whole world once and for all who God's chosen people were by putting them above all other nations. They were too self-focused to realize that being God's chosen people meant that the savior of all nations was to come from within their own nation.

They may very well have ridiculed the dozens of others who claimed to be the long-awaited Messiah but just ended up arrested, crucified, or dying during rebellions against Roman soldiers.

They lived under the Pharisee's interpretation of God's law. That law, given by God as guidelines for the best way to live, had become oppressive under the Pharisee's control. For example: people worried that they might spill some grain on the ground which might then take root and sprout, making them guilty of planting something (working) on the Sabbath.

They lived under constant fear of accidentally breaking a rule, which they thought would bring God's wrath down upon them.

The disdain and ridicule levied against Jesus may not have been personal attacks, but instead anger and frustration about what he represented: hope of relief from Roman tyranny dying with a common, Jewish troublemaker. For many, of course, it was anger that someone who clearly was not the Messiah had claimed to be so; in their minds, the very fact that he was on a cross proved that he was not the true Messiah.

We see the same kind of vitriol levied against Christ-followers today. Today the ridicule comes from many directions and for many reasons, but we'll focus on three. First, people attack Christianity because they have been physically or emotionally hurt, lied to, deceived, spiritually abused, or otherwise harmed by someone associated with the faith, and they project their feelings about that person onto all Christians. Second, people attack Christianity because they see the examples in the Bible of Christ serving, loving, sacrificing—yet it seems that most of his followers are only focused on themselves. In other words, the Christians they have experienced are hypocrites, so they assume all Christians are hypocrites, and the entire faith is full of hypocrisy. Third, people may attack Christianity because they are jealous or envious. They see in Christians what they desire but don't think they can have for themselves – peace, hope, belonging to a loving community, the assurance of forgiveness, certainty that there is more to life than just the material world, answers to the big questions of life – but instead of embracing Christianity they attack and demean what they think they can't have. It's like teenage boys who say Justin Bieber is a loser and a jerk; it's not that they know Bieber to be unpleasant, but they are jealous of his looks, his success, his car, and all the attention he gets.

Many other people are apathetic toward Christianity, not necessarily calling it a pack of lies, but rather seeing it as pointless, useless, and ineffective. Apparently, such persons have never witnessed anyone truly and effectively living the Christian life. This is why we see the following quotes (both misattributed to Gandhi) so often:
- "I like your Christ. I do not like your Christians. They are so unlike your Christ."

Notes:

Notes:

- "Jesus is ideal and wonderful, but you Christians—you are not like him."

Theological Underpinnings

There really is no excuse for anyone to observe how a Christian lives and not understand that Christianity is about God first, others second, and self third. Our Confession of Faith clearly states that the church never exists for itself alone (5.09), but that believers are to share with nonbelievers the good news of the possibility of salvation through Jesus Christ (5.28, 5.30).

Somehow, though, we have made church and Christianity about ourselves first and God second, often leaving it there and not including anyone else. Evangelism and growing the church roll are seen as synonymous. Financial planning budgets for the members' needs first, only giving leftovers – if any – to outreach efforts. And when money gets tight, outreach efforts are the first things to be cut. Wars have been fought between groups who have different ideas about Christianity. Opposing sides in military and social conflict have both claimed their positions to be Christ-like. So, in many instances, those who ridicule Christianity have good reason to do so. No Christian or church congregation should be expected to be perfectly Christ-like all the time, but many of us can do much, much better.

The best way to reach those who assume Christianity is a waste of time, and those who openly ridicule our faith, is by showing them the truth and strength of Christianity by living out our faith and love on a daily basis, not just for two hours on a Sunday morning.

Applying the Lesson to Your Own Life

Is there someone you dislike, even though you can't honestly say why? If so, could it be that they have something you wish you had?

Are you apathetic about certain things, ideas, or social movements—having dismissed them as worthless without really knowing much about them?

When you participate in, or support outreach efforts, do you do it for the benefit of others or to feel good?

Recall a time you encountered someone apathetic or hostile toward Christianity. How did you react? Are you pleased with that? Do you think God was pleased? If not, what could you have done better? If you've never had such an experience, how do you think you would react?

Put yourself in the place of someone who knows nothing about Jesus or Christianity: how complete a picture of the faith would that person get from observing you for a couple of days, excluding Sunday?

The Lesson

Get Started (10 min.)

Before class gather as wide a variety of art supplies as you can, but keep the art supplies out of sight.

Begin the lesson by helping your students adopt a serious, introspective mood. Have everyone close their eyes and take a few deep breaths.

Say: *Think about a time that somebody made fun of you… in public. Not in a playful way, but really trying to hurt your feelings and embarrass you. Recall how that made you feel.*

Don't ask or allow students to share their stories, but give them a moment to recall such an incident and recapture their feelings at the time.

Say: *Now think about a time you were telling somebody the truth about something important, but they didn't believe you and said you were lying.*

Again, don't ask or allow students to share their stories, but give them a moment to recall such an incident and recapture their feelings at the time. Don't rush them.

Notes:

Notes:

When all students indicate they have remembered or re-captured their feelings during such incidents, dump all the art supplies in a central location. If that doesn't make your student open their eyes, invite them to. It's okay if you make a mess. Your students' feelings should be kind of messy too at this point.

Say: *Make something to visually display how you felt when these things happened.*

Don't offer help too quickly, but if you have a student who thinks all art has to look like something (people, trees, buildings), and that attitude is keeping her from doing this exercise, gently encourage her to use colors or textures (rather than shapes or figures) to express what she wants to.

Allow plenty of time to work. Give "time left" updates every two minutes.

When time is up, leave the art supplies out and move on to the next part of the lesson. Students will need their artwork later. If you think your students can continue working but still pay attention to the lesson, consider allowing them to do so. Resist the urge to clean up any mess, and if you're blessed enough to have students who like to tidy up, ask them to wait.

Listen Up (20 min.)

Have students read aloud Mark 15:29-30 from several different translations of the Bible. If you do not have different translations available, go to www.biblegateway.com before class so you can search and print several translations.

Suggested:
- Contemporary English Version,
- English Standard Version,
- God's Word Translation,
- King James Version,
- The Message,
- New American Standard Bible,
- New Century Version,

- New International Version,
- New King James Version,
- New Living Translation,
- New Revised Standard Version,
- The Voice.

If you have a small class, have each student read more than one translation.

When the Bibles have been put down, invite students to look at the artwork they have just made.

Say: *As Jesus hung on a cross beside the road -- naked, bleeding, beaten nearly to death -- people walking by shook their heads, hurled insults and abuse at him, ridiculed him, laughed at him, said terrible things about him, and made fun of the most important thing in the world to him.*

Pause for a few seconds.

Reflection Question:
- Might your artwork show how Jesus felt in those moments?

Don't allow responses; just spend a moment in silence with everyone contemplating this question.

Ask students to respond to this quote from G.K. Chesterton in *What's Wrong with the World*:
> "The Christian ideal has not been tried and found wanting. It has been found difficult; and left untried."

You may want to write it on the board or newsprint.

Since this quote uses some slightly archaic language, decide if your students will fully understand it. If necessary, explain that "ideal" here is not an adjective, but a noun meaning a concept in its perfect state. "Wanting" does not mean desiring something, but rather lacking something. "Tried" does not mean attempted in the first sentence, but instead tested or examined with close scrutiny.

Break the class into pairs. Ensure each pair has a fresh piece of paper and something to write with. Ask each pair to re-write the Chesterton quote in their own words. Allow a few minutes for this; then have each pair join up with another pair. These quartets are to alter, or combine their two new quotes into one new quote that will restate Chesterton's

Notes:

Notes:

quote. Continue this pattern until you have only two groups, and then have the whole class decide on which new quote best contemporizes the Chesterton quote.

Have someone write the new, consensus quote on the board or on newsprint.

Discuss the following question:
- G.K. Chesterton wrote that original quote way back in 1910. Is it still true today?
    - [If so] What makes being a Christian so difficult today?
    - [If not] What makes being a Christian easy today?

- Two thousand years ago, people laughed at Jesus. Do people still make fun of, and ridicule, Christianity?
    - [If so] Why do you think they do?
    - [If not] What changed?

- Do people today actively and intentionally work against Christianity?
    - [If so] Why do you think they do so?

- How might you react to someone who said Christianity is a big waste of time?
- How might you react to someone who said Christianity is a bunch of lies believed only by idiots?
- What might happen if one of these people who is apathetic toward Christianity, or actively opposed to Christianity, were to see somebody-- somebody like one of us -- truly living a Christ-like life?

Now What? (15 min.)

Indicate the pile of art supplies. Have your students make another work of art. This piece of artwork is to be the exact opposite of their first work, reflecting what it's like to be accepted, wanted, believed, welcomed, affirmed.

Give students plenty of time to work on this, and then call a stop. Have students look at their own work and ask: Might your artwork show how Jesus feels every time somebody formerly opposed to him believes in him, accepts the forgiveness he made possible, and makes him the most important thing in their life?

Spend a moment in silence allowing students to reflect on this.

 ## Live It (5 min.)

Indicate the messiness of the room and say something like: Just like this room is a mess, it was a mess at the cross that day… but not a hopeless mess. Sometimes our lives are a mess… but never a hopeless mess. God cleaned up the messiness of the cross by turning it into something good. In the same way, God can clean up the messiest life by turning the mess into something good.

Start cleaning up the mess in your classroom.

Say: *And when we work with God to clean up the mess in our own lives, how we live will show others -- even those who are full of anger or apathy toward Christianity -- that Christ is real… and good… and that he loves them.*

Continue cleaning up, enlisting the students' help, until you can all stand and look at the clean room. Close the class with a prayer like this: Life is messy, God. Use us to show the world that, through Jesus, you can clean up even the biggest mess.

Resources used: *Seven Words of Men Around the Cross*, by Paul Moore

© 2014 Discipleship Ministry Team of the Ministry Council of the Cumberland Presbyterian Church. All Rights Reserved.

Notes:

Here is Your Son.
Here is Your Mother.
by Jennifer Newell

Scripture: John 19:26

Theme: At the end of his earthly ministry, Jesus creates a family united by their love for Jesus and for each other.

Resource List

- Bibles or printed copies of the scripture passages you'll be using.
- Masking tape
- Copy of each question from "Call to Wake Up" (so you can tape one question to each student's back)
- "Coat of Arms" worksheet for each student
- Markers or pencils
- Sharpie marker (thin or medium point would work best)
- Music player (laptop, iPod, MP3 player, CD player, speakers, etc.)
- Recording of "We Are Family" by Sister Sledge
- Display lyrics for "We are Family"
- Digital camera
- Optional: pictures of the women your group will "adopt" as "Church Moms."
- White board or sheets of newsprint
- Marker

Leader Prep

- For "Family of Mine" Activity: Identify women in the church who your youth could "adopt" as Church Moms. They can be old or young, single or married—but they can't be the actual mothers (or stepmothers) of anyone in your group. Explain to these prospective "adoptees" the importance of helping the church's youth feel more deeply connected to their larger church family. Your group will work together to come up with ways to build relationships with their adopted Church Moms.
- Your CPWM is an excellent resource for this activity.
- Family Portraits: You might want to create a classic "portrait" area using formal chairs, a couch, or even potted plants. Students could also do this on their smart phones.

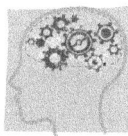

Leader Insight

Connecting to Your Students
When we talk about family, we often talk in idealized terms. We allude to a nearly perfect family that is supportive, healthy, and whole.

Your students probably don't have that sort of family. Disease,

Notes:

addiction, and divorce disrupt family life. Financial strain, obligations to extended family, and our overly-busy work and extracurricular lives add to the stresses placed on families today. As you go through the lesson, be sensitive to your students' own family situations.

Flip through your Bible. It isn't full of idealized families either. Cain and Abel, the first set of brothers, quickly became the world's first murderer and murder victim. Abraham banished his son Ishmael to the desert; Joseph's brothers sold him into slavery; Jacob worked with his mother to trick his father and cheat his brother out of a blessing; one of David's sons raped his own sister; and another led a rebellion against his father. African-American ministers have been encouraged to do everything they can to ensure that youth have "the home court advantage." All of us need someone to cheer us on, to celebrate our successes, to inspire us to be heroic, and to offer loving correction when we mess up.

The church has an obligation to step-in when biological families are not able to offer support, stability, encouragement, and guidance. This week, prayerfully consider ways that your church and your ministry can provide the "home court advantage" your youth so desperately need.

Explaining the Bible

John's Gospel offers no account of Jesus' birth or early life. However, John's account of Jesus' public ministry is book-ended by scenes which involve his mother.

The first story takes place in John 2. Jesus and his mother are guests at a wedding in Cana. Mary points out to her son that the hosts have run out of wine (a very embarrassing situation), and he says—and not too politely, it would seem—"what is that to you and me?"

"Woman, my time has not come," he says, which is not the sort of answer you'd expect. Mary does not fully understand this son of hers, but she knows one thing: if you want to get something done, pay attention to what he says. "Do whatever he tells you," she informs the servants, and Jesus' miracle is now in full swing. The wine is flowing, the party is saved, and Jesus' public ministry has begun.

At a wedding, when the hosts were in a predicament, Jesus rebuked his mother by declaring that his "time had not yet come."

But just a couple of years later, it had (see John 13:1, 17:1). His "time" has come—the reason for everything, the point of his existence. His time has come, and it is here and now: on this cross, in this pain, facing this certain and unpleasant death. And Mary no more understands this situation in John 19, than she did his odd words at Cana.

Her relationship with Jesus doesn't hinge on whether or not she understands him completely. She is his mother, forever linked to him by the bonds of love. The ministry that started at a party with his mother looks like it will end here, on the cross, with his mother standing close by.

"Woman," says Jesus. "Here is your son."

The word translated "here" in the NRSV is rendered "behold" in other translations. In order to emphasize the importance of what Jesus is doing, we'll make use of the word "behold" throughout the lesson.

"Behold" is a powerful word—a word of revelation. It isn't a suggestion; it's a command. Look carefully. Pay attention. Open your eyes to something you have never noticed before. It's used hundreds of times in the New Testament. Clearly, two things are true: (1) we need to pay attention to what God is up to, and (2) we are easily distracted from God's revelations and interventions!

When Jesus leaves his mother and the beloved disciple in one another's care, he creates a new family. This new family isn't based on shared DNA, but on a shared love of Jesus. Jesus loves them, and they love him. Now he's asking them, for his sake and theirs, to love one another.

In essence, this is the first church family. This church family, small though it was—not quite sure of its theology just yet, and totally without any committee structure at all (can you imagine?!)—was held together by a bond that made it strong and resilient: a shared relationship with Jesus Christ.

When the chips were down, troubles were mounting, and the shadow of death was hanging over them, these two broken-hearted people banded together and acted like a family for each other. In their shared love for Christ, they reached out and loved one another.

"And from that hour," John tells us, "the disciple took her into his own home" (John 19:27).

Notes:

Notes:

The phrase "into his own" is the same one used at the beginning of John's Gospel: "[Jesus] came to what was his own, and his own people did not accept him" (John 1:11). It's used again in John 16:32, where Jesus predicts that, when trouble comes, the disciples "will be scattered, each one to his home." Using this phrase again reinforces the idea of a mission that has been completed: what was broken has been made whole. Unlike the world that "did not accept" Christ, and unlike the other disciples who quickly sought refuge in their own homes, the beloved disciples accepts Mary as family, and she finds a home with him.

Our lesson today helps us see Jesus' words to Mary as an affirmation of relationships and a mandate to the new community of faith, which has been commanded to show their commitment to God through their love for one another (John 13:34-35).

Theological Underpinnings

As you examine today's scripture, be careful not to allude to Mary as a "sainted," perfect mother, because Scripture tells us otherwise. She did not always understand Jesus, and her desires for him sometimes put her at odds with his God-given mission. Recall the episode where she lost track of him on their pilgrimage to the Temple (Luke 2:41-51); their conversation at the Wedding at Cana (John 2); and her attempts to take him back home because he seemed to be "out of his mind" (Mark 3:21). We identify best with Mary as a fully human mother, not as a flawless "super saint."

The image of the church as a family permeates the New Testament. In the Gospels, and in the writings of Peter, Paul, and John, the community of believers is referred to repeatedly as "children" of God, "brothers and sisters" in Christ, and even a "family of faith."

Our Confession of Faith addresses the community of believers as a family. "God acts to restore sinful persons to a covenant relationship, the nature of which is that of a family" (Confession of Faith, 3.02). Once saved, we are welcomed into "community with God and with one's brothers and sisters in Christ, both now and in the full redemption of the family of God" (Confession of Faith, 4.20).

Today's lesson gives us the opportunity to consider what it means to be a family of faith. As brothers and sisters, what is our obligation toward one another? How does shared faith change the nature of our relationships?

Applying the Lesson to Your Own Life

Aging is inevitable. We grow up, and our parents grow old. Once upon a time, you needed your parents in order to survive each day; as they grow older, your parents will need you. The command to honor our parents is a life-long responsibility. Roles shift, but the relationship remains. As you prepare for this lesson, consider your relationship with your parents. How has it changed since you were a teen? In what ways do you still need your parents? In what ways might they need you?

Another aspect of this story is that Jesus provides support for his mother by enlisting the help of someone else he could trust. Are there other trusted care-providers in your parents' lives? If so, take time this week to thank them, and to thank God for them.

The Lesson

Get Started (12 min.)

Call to Worship: Assign readers for each of the verses below, asking them to emphasize the words in bold. Explain that each verse contains the Greek word eido, which is usually translated "here," "see," or "look" in the NRSV. In many other translations, though, it is rendered "behold." The word "behold" is not a word we use in normal conversation, but it is powerful imperative and it will help us focus on the surprising, and even radical, work of God within the family of faith.

As each verse is read, the group will respond with an energetic "BEHOLD!" You might want to practice this a few times until the group has enthusiasm. You might even want to add a hand motion to emphasize just how powerful a word this is.

READER 1: "Do not be afraid; for **see**—I am bringing you good news of great joy for all the people." (Luke 2:10b)

Notes:

Notes:

ALL:	BEHOLD!
READER 2:	"Here is the Lamb of God who takes away the sin of the world!" (John 1:29)
ALL:	BEHOLD!
READER 3:	"Look, your king is coming, sitting on a donkey's colt!" (John 12:15b)
ALL:	BEHOLD!
READER 4:	"Get up, let us be going," said Jesus. "See, my betrayer is at hand." (Matthew 26:46)
ALL:	BEHOLD!
READER 5:	"Do not be alarmed; you are looking for Jesus of Nazareth, who was crucified. He has been raised; he is not here. Look, there is the place they laid him." (Mark 16:6)
ALL:	BEHOLD!

Call to Wake Up

Tape one of the questions listed below on each student's back. No one should know what question is on their own back. As students mingle, they should answer the question (or fill in the blank) without revealing what the question is. At the end of the activity, each student will guess what question is taped to his/her back.

These questions are related (if only tangentially!) to today's lesson. They'll serve as a jumping-off point for your discussion of the passage by helping students think about mothers, families, and Jesus' death.

- Define a good mom.
- If you saw Jesus on the cross, what would you say to him?
- What's another word for "behold?"
- Name someone in the church who is like family to you (but not related to you).
- How would you feel if you saw a person being crucified?
- Name a type of relative (brother, granny, etc.).
- Name one thing a "good kid" does to help his/her parents.
- Name one thing you and your mother have in common.
- Your mother's middle name is.

Listen Up (20 min.)

Setting the Stage

Divide students into three groups. Each group should read John 19:16-27, and then help set the scene as directed below. After the groups have had a few minutes to brainstorm and prepare, have them share their sights, sounds, and emotions as you read (slowly and dramatically) through the Scripture passage.

Group 1: SEE IT: What would you have seen if you had been present during the events of this passage? Create at least three visual props for the scene. You can draw them, make them out of found items, or use group members to create them.

Group 2: HEAR IT: What might you have heard if you had been present during the events of this passage? As a group, create at least three sound effects for this passage.

Group 3: FEEL IT: What sort of emotions are the people in this passage likely feeling? Make a list; then choose at least three of these emotions to act out.

After you have read the passage (complete with the groups embellishments), move on to the heart of the lesson.

Digging into the Scripture

Say: *Today's lesson is about one tiny part of the story we just shared. It's a detail found only in John's Gospel—and it is one of the rare times in John's Gospel where Jesus' mother is on the scene.*

Some commentators say that Mary and the other women could be at the cross because, as women, they were so unimportant no one cared about who they associated with. Surely they weren't the first group of teary-eyed women to stand and cry at the foot of a cross.

But don't write off that group of women too quickly; those women were there out of devotion, loyalty, compassion, and

Notes:

Notes:

Notes:

love, and we see in them a love that is a real force to be reckoned with. Other people are at the cross just doing their jobs (the soldiers) or in order to taunt the dying men, but these women are there out of love. This is love that trumps fear; love that wades into uncomfortable places; love that keeps its eyes wide open when so many others would have turned their heads.

Jesus is in pain now, but his pain is almost over; Mary is the one that will have to live with it. Despite his own pain, Jesus reaches out to her in love. Jesus asks his mother and this disciple to look at one another and relate to one another in a new way. "Woman," he says, "here is your son." And then he turns to a disciple identified only by Jesus' love for him, and says, "here is your mother."

Discussion Questions:
- How does the fact that Jesus' Mom watched him suffer and die make you feel? How would you feel about the story if not even his mother had been there?
- Why do you think the disciple is unnamed? What does that add to our experience of this story?

Say: *The fact that Jesus' mother was at the cross reminds us of Jesus' humanity: he was a real person, flesh and blood, with a real mother whom he really loved. He really hurt, he really suffered, and he really died.*

Jesus was taking care of his mother, but he was also showing us a new way to think about family. Instead of defining "family" in terms of marriage laws, DNA, and last names, Jesus defines family as people who have a shared commitment to God. That shared commitment to God gives us a special relationship with each other.

Have volunteers read the following verses.
1. Matthew 12:49-50: And pointing to his disciples, [Jesus] said, "Here are my mother and my brothers! For whoever does the will of my Father in heaven is my brother and sister and mother."
2. 1 John 3:1: See what love the Father has given us, that we should be called children of God; and that is what we are.
3. 1 Timothy 5:1-2: Do not speak harshly to an older man, but speak to him as to a father, to younger men as brothers, to older women as mothers, to younger women as sisters—with absolute purity.

Discussion Questions:
- What do these verses tell us about our church family?
- As a family, how should we treat each other? What other Bible passages can you think of that might help us figure that out?
- What sort of things do people in your church do that create "family" in your congregation? When bad things happen, how does the church respond? When good things happen, how does the church celebrate? Try to list as many things as you can think of.

Now What? (15 min.)

Family of Mine

Work with your CPWM before-hand to identify women in the congregation who your youth can "adopt" as church moms. If possible, have pictures of these women on-hand. Together, brainstorm about ways that your group can be family to these women. How can your group benefit from getting to know them? How can those women benefit from building a relationship with members of your group? Plan an event that brings the two groups together. Include some sort of ice-breaker activity and some way to exchange information between the two groups. Commit to praying for one another for a set period of time.

Coat of Arms

Using the worksheet provided, have students create a coat of arms for their church family. They may want to include symbols of their church's ministries; symbols that represent core beliefs or practices of their congregation; or symbols that represent the ways church members love and care for one another. At the top of the worksheet is a space for a motto. This could be a Bible verse, your church's mission or vision statement, or a short motto that seems to summarize your church's identity.

Just in Case:

We are Family!

Look up the lyrics to "We are Family" by Sister Sledge (they are easy to find online), and print them out. Play the song, then talk about how you could re-write those lyrics as a theme song for your church family. Encourage the students to come up with lyrics that are scripturally sound and convey the joy of being a church family.

Just in Case:

Family Portrait

Have groups of students pose for classic family portraits. If other people are available at church during your meeting time, include them, too. If you meet during Sunday School, the youth could travel to different classes and groups and take their "family portraits." Print the portraits and display them throughout the church, or download them onto your church's website. For an extra "punch," ask the students to come up with captions that add to the "family" element in these pictures (example: "the family that prays together stays together," or "they'll know we are Christians by our love").

Live It (5 min.)

Role Models

There is an old African proverb that says, "It takes a village to raise a child." The idea is this: when it comes to helping kids grow up, all sorts of people have a role to play. Coaches and teachers; scout leaders and neighbors; church family and friends: all of these people have the opportunity to influence kids' lives in good ways, no matter what their last name happens to be.

Have the class make a group list of all the people they can think of who have nurtured and encouraged them. What sort of things have these people done to be helpful and supportive?

As older youth, little kids look up to you. What sort of role model are you for them? How can you support, encourage, and nurture the little kids who are watching you? Brainstorm ways you can share God's love with younger kids this week. Close with a prayer of thanksgiving for our family of faith, asking for God's grace and God's help as we learn more about what it means to be family for each other.

Brothers and Sisters

Have the students stand in a circle. Give one student a Sharpie marker. Have that student draw a small heart on the palm of the student to his/her left, and say, "(name): you are my brother/sister."

The student with the marker then passes the marker to the left, and the process repeats until the entire circle has participated. When the entire group has been marked, link arms and lead the group in a very short prayer that asks God to help us live as brothers and sisters.

© 2014 Discipleship Ministry Team of the Ministry Council of the Cumberland Presbyterian Church. All Rights Reserved.

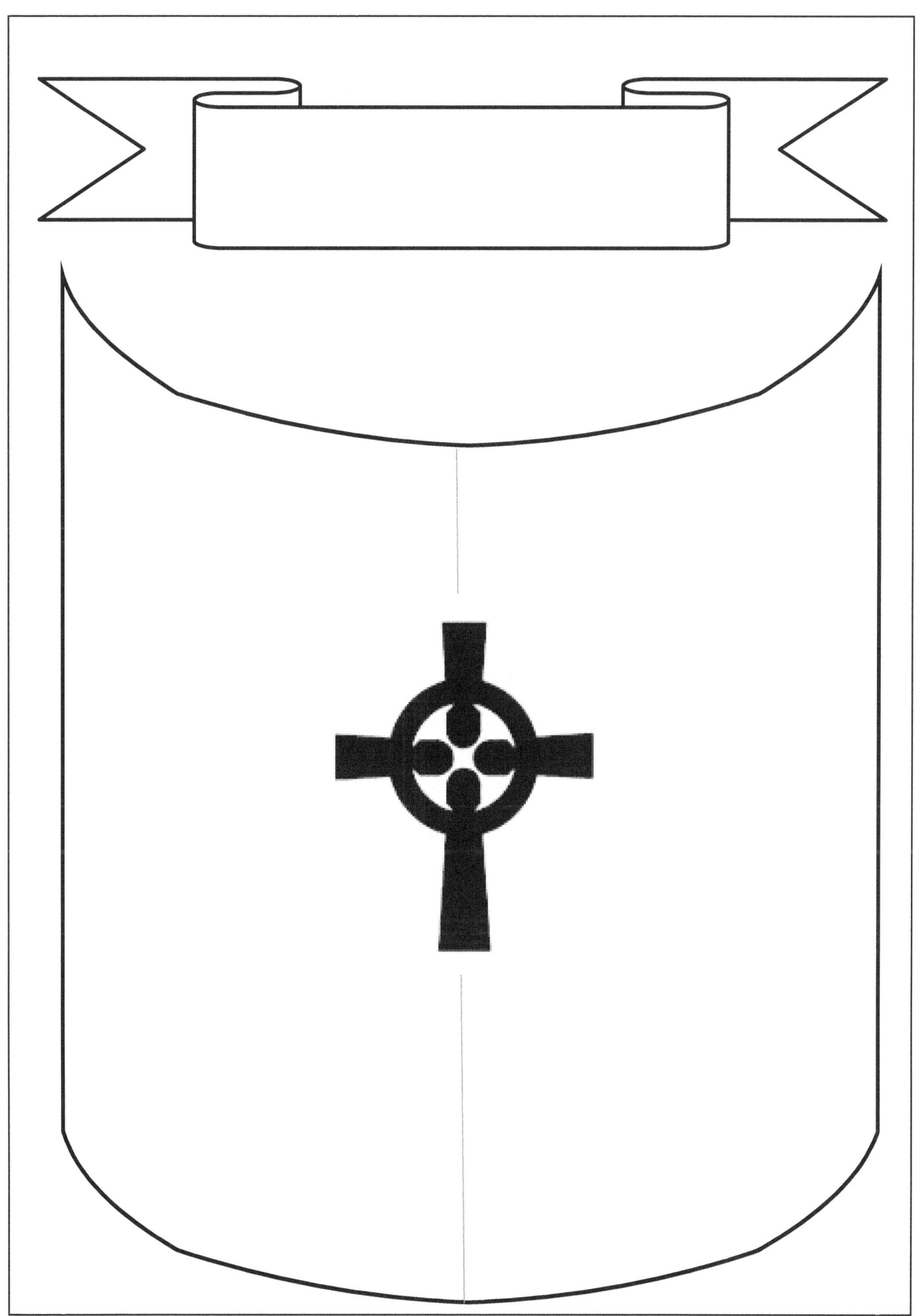

BEHOLD!

READER 1:
"Do not be afraid; for see—I am bringing you good news of great joy for all the people." (Luke 2:10b)

ALL:
BEHOLD!

READER 2:
"Here is the Lamb of God who takes away the sin of the world!" (John 1:29)

ALL:
BEHOLD!

READER 3:
"Look, your king is coming, sitting on a donkey's colt!" (John 12:15b)

ALL:
BEHOLD!

READER 4:
"Get up, let us be going," said Jesus. "See, my betrayer is at hand." (Matthew 26:46)

ALL:
BEHOLD!

READER 5:
"Do not be alarmed; you are looking for Jesus of Nazareth, who was crucified. He has been raised; he is not here. Look, there is the place they laid him." (Mark 16:6)

ALL:
BEHOLD!

He Can't Save Himself
by Andy McClung

Scripture: Mark 15:31-32

Theme: What do we do when those in authority attack our faith?

Resource List

- Newsprint or marker board
- Markers
- Improv Theater A and B handouts

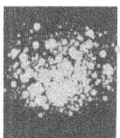

Leader Prep

- Photocopy the two handout sheets: Improv Theatre A and B. Cut apart the three scene setups for each.
- For the Listen Up section, you might want to look up the names of elected officials for your city and state before class to help with this. Check http://whoismy-representative.com/ and http://www.usa.gov/Contact/Elected.shtml before class for help in this. Depending on your location, you may have students from different political districts.

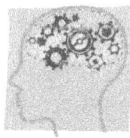

Leader Insight

Connecting to Your Students
It's often assumed that teens are rebellious against authority figures, especially their parents. Research shows that while conflicts between teens and their parents do increase for a couple of years in early adolescence, such conflicts usually focus on relatively minor issues (personal appearance, household rules), and most teens actually agree with their parents on the important issues (faith, morals). The whole "teenage rebellion" thing is just a repetition of toddlers wanting -- and needing -- to do for themselves things for which they previ

Notes:

ously relied on others. It's not cute when teens do it, though. It's frustrating. Those couple of years can seem like an eternity for parents.

Teens get tired of hearing how rebellious they are. Challenging authority is one way they learn how to make autonomous, responsible, adult decisions. Instead of griping about it, we should help teens learn how to appropriately challenge authority. Because sometimes authority figures need to be challenged.

Explaining the Bible
Although Mark 15:29-32, is written as one scene in which Jesus is mocked and derided while he hangs on the cross, Mark makes it clear that verses 29-30 depict commoners mocking Jesus (covered in another lesson in this series), and verses 31-32 depict the chief priests deriding Jesus(covered in this lesson). This is an important distinction.

In First Century Jewish society, religion, economics, politics, and culture were all inseparably intertwined, and most people were either rich or poor; there was almost no middle class. The chief priests were the elite of that society. They gained their positions by being the descendants of Aaron, Moses' older brother who stood beside Moses throughout the exodus and held up Moses' arms during the crossing of the Red Sea. Aaron was the first high priest and also the one who let the people talk him into making the Golden Calf. So, even with the very first high priest, we see the inherent limitations of a normal human acting as mediator between humanity and God.

In Jesus' day, high priests were still the mediators between God and humankind; they represented the people before God and served as God's ambassadors to the people. What they said was taken as God's direct words. They were the only ones who could enter the Temple's inner most part – the Holy of Holies, where the Ark of the Covenant was kept and where the Jews believed God resided – to make a sacrifice each year on the Day of Atonement. They also controlled the temple's finances, which were substantial since every Jewish citizen was expected to give one-tenth of his income to God through the Temple. The priests, through the temple system, also made money when worshipers purchased animals to sacrifice, and when worshipers from outside of Jerusalem exchanged their money for local money to buy sacrificial animals. Being a Jewish priest in the First Century could be lucrative and definitely was a position of power. Jesus threat-

ened this power by offering a different path to God, a way to have a personal relationship with God through Christ.
For this lesson, let's note three things about the chief priests' taunts in Mark 15:31-32.

First, despite the words they used, they were not seriously hoping Jesus would come down from the cross and prove himself to be the Messiah. Mark knows tone and inflection are a big part of how we communicate, so he is sure to let us know that they were mocking Jesus.

Second, they challenged Jesus to come down from the cross. They probably meant it only in a literal sense: "Remove yourself from up there (the cross) and stand down here (on the ground with us)." There is also, however, a figurative meaning behind their words which they probably didn't intend: "We aren't spiritual enough; we aren't close enough to God; we don't know God well enough to come up to your level of spirituality, so if we are going to meet anywhere, you're going to have to come down to our level." That is exactly what God had done in becoming human; these chief priests had just missed it.

Third, they challenged Jesus to save himself because that's the only thing that might possibly make them believe in him. This reveals their utter self-centeredness. In their minds taking care of oneself is the most important thing in the world. They seem to be incapable of even conceiving that Jesus might prove he was Messiah by staying on the cross and dying for the sake of others. Or, because people in authority are used to making rules and they expect others to obey those rules, maybe the chief priests thought even God would have to obey their words.

Whether it's a small book club, a congregation, or an entire nation, leaders set the tone for the organizations they lead. This is true even if members of the organizations don't unanimously agree with every decision the leaders make. The leaders of a Cumberland Presbyterian congregation are the session: the pastor and the elders. They set the tone for the whole congregation. That's why electing good elders -- spiritually mature, able to listen for God instead of assuming what God wants, steeped in Cumberland Presbyterian doctrine and polity, mission-minded, respected in the community, active in the life of the church beyond the local congregation -- is vital to the life and ministry of a Cumberland Presbyterian church. Just as teenagers sometimes learn to make their own decisions by questioning, or even challenging, the authority of

Notes:

Notes:

their parents or teachers, congregations sometimes only grow by questioning or challenging the authority of a session which is making decisions that lead the congregation away from God's will or accepted Cumberland Presbyterian theology.

Theological Underpinnings
We attack things we fear. Sometimes these attacks are violent in an attempt to get rid of what scares us. Sometimes theses attacks take the form of ridiculing what scares us to make

it seem unimportant or foolish. The people in authority in Jesus' day took both approaches. They violently killed Jesus because he threatened their power, and they ridiculed him to make his message seem foolish.

Christianity has always been made fun of. Brutal violence has been, and continues to be, committed against Christians. And it doesn't seem as if things are going to get any better anytime soon. In fact, they'll probably get worse.

Authority figures who attack, work against, or ridicule Christianity do so, in part, because they fear it. Christianity puts all authority in God, not in those leaders or in the systems they create to maintain power.

Cumberland Presbyterians believe that those with authority have the responsibility to make whatever system they work in a way of enacting God's will in the world. This applies to the pastor and elders who are in authority over the congregation, the presbytery which is authority over ministers and sessions, and synods and the General Assembly that are in authority over presbyteries. Our church government is designed to make doing ministry an organized and effective endeavor (see Preamble to the CP Constitution). According to our Confession of Faith, civil government, though created by humans, is supposed to make the world like God wants it. Christians have the duty to support government when it does this and to challenge government when it doesn't. According to our Confession of Faith and the US Constitution, the government cannot be in complete authority over the Church (Confession of Faith 6.27-6.32).

Applying the Lesson to Your Own Life
Do you think the chief priests went out and personally taunted all of the crucified false messiahs, or was this something they reserved for Jesus?

Which has a stronger effect on how you live your life: being a Christian or being a citizen of your country? How are the two in harmony? How are they in conflict? If it came down to choosing one over the other, with which would you side?

Do you question authority?

If so: How? Is it a common or rare situation? What's it take to make you move from questioning authority to challenging it? How do you ensure that your questioning and challenging is productive rather than just complaining? Is there one source of authority you're more/less likely to question or challenge than others?

If not: Why not? Is it apathy? Fear of backlash? What would it take to make you question authority? To challenge authority?

The Lesson

Get Started (10 min.)

Choose several students to read aloud, one by one, the ten items from the "Real News or Not?" handout. After each story is read, have the entire class vote on whether they think it really happened, or if it's made up. Majority wins, but ask some questions to get your students thinking— especially when there is a split vote. For example: Why don't you think that's true? What makes you think that this really happened? Is there a certain part that sounds fishy to you? You don't seem sure how to vote, what's your hesitancy about?

Have one student, on newsprint or marker board, keep a record of the prevailing vote for each item. For example: #1 = real, #2 = not real.

After all of the news items have been read aloud and voted on, say you're going to go back through them one by one

Notes:

Notes:

and reveal whether or not each is real. Then pretend to change your mind and say something like: *Well, to save some time let's just do it this way: all those stories are real, and they all happened recently.*

Move right into the next part of this lesson.

Listen Up (15 min.)

Discussion Question:
- What do all those stories have in common? (This is referring to the "Real News or Not?" handout.) You may, of course, get several different answers, but if necessary, guide your students to recognize that the source of the poor treatment of Christians were all authority figures.

Leader Tip:
Maybe a leading question would help them reach this conclusion, such as: Right, they all involve Christians being treated poorly, and who was treating them poorly? What do all of the abusers in these stories have in common? Affirm good or close answers with something like: Right! They were all people in authority.

Have students name as many positions of authority as they can. You're looking for titles or positions, not personal names at this point. Anything is fair game: from parents to police, from pastor to president, from principal to senator. Have a student write these titles on the newsprint or board, leaving some space beside each title. If students don't offer them, suggest adding city council members, county aldermen, state representatives, etc.

Once you've run out of space or responses, go back to each title/position and have students list as many names as they can under each position.

Discussion Question:
- From a Christian perspective, what decisions have some of these people made, or what actions have they taken, that you believe are good?

Leader Tip:
You may have to be ready with a few hints yourself. For example: "Remember last year when the city council..."

Have the student doing the writing summarize the responses on the board/sheet and mark it as a good thing, maybe by using a "+" symbol.

You can find out how your US congressman voted on any particular law at www.senate.gov and www.house.gov.

Discussion Question:
- From a Christian perspective, what decisions have some of these people made, or what actions have they taken, that you believe are not good?

Have the student doing the writing summarize the responses on the board/sheet and mark it as a bad thing, maybe by using a "-" symbol.

Have someone read aloud Mark 15:31-32.

Share what you think appropriate and useful from the background information about the chief priests who made fun of Jesus.

Say: *From the very beginning of Christianity, some leaders and people in authority have been hostile toward our faith. There are good ways, and bad ways, to respond when someone in power attacks your faith.*

Discussion Questions:
- What would be a bad way to respond to, let's say [draw a "-" example from the board].
- What would be a better way to respond?

Say: *Being in a position of power is a lot of responsibility. Sometimes it's hard for leaders to do things that are good from a Christian perspective. When they do, it's helpful for them to hear "thank you."*

Discussion Question:
- What would be a good way to say 'thank you' for, let's say [draw a positive example from the board].

After you have heard some good ideas, ask each student to choose two of the items written on the board, one positive and one negative. They are to e-mail, phone, or write to the persons involved, saying "thank you" to the positive items, and/or to express displeasure at the negative items... all from a Christian perspective.

Be sure to help students find the appropriate contact information. Also encourage them to be respectful and concise in their writing or speaking. Mentioning their age is important.

They probably should not mention this lesson directly, but should emphasize that they are responding – either positively or negatively – from a Christian perspective.

Notes:

Leader Tip:
You may have to be ready with a few hints yourself. For example: "Remember last year when the school board..."

Notes:

Now What? (20 min.)

Announce that the class will now enjoy some "improv" theatre. If someone doesn't know what this is, explain that it is acting without using scripts or holding rehearsals – improvising what is said and done on the spot.

For the first scene, either ask for two volunteers or just choose two students to be the actors. Give the student who is to play the authority figure "Improv Theatre Scene Setup #1A". Give the student who will be playing himself or herself "Improv Theatre Scene Setup #1B". Allow one minute for them to look over the scene setup.

While they do this, explain to the class that one of the actors will be playing a completely fictitious role while the other is basically playing himself/herself, but in a fictional situation. Very briefly introduce each scene for the class' benefit before telling the actors to begin.

> Scene #1 [B's name] is a teenager who has just started working at Burger Bucket, a fast food restaurant. [A's name] is his/her manager and boss.
>
> Scene #2 [B's name] is on the middle school synchronized swimming team. [A's name] is his/her coach. The team is just about to hit the pool for a big competition against their toughest rivals, The Orange County Otters.
>
> Scene #3 [B's name] is a college student on the first day of a new semester. He/she is sitting in a class with a professor he/she has never had before [A's name] is his/her professor.

Either the actors, or you, will have to decide when each scene is over. You should stop the scene if there is silence for more than twenty seconds, if it's obvious the actors are out of ideas, or if the actors stray too far from the point.

This portion of the lesson could go very quickly or take far too long, depending on how much your students get into it. If you need to stretch out this exercise, just repeat one or more of the scenes using different actors, make up your own scenes to present to the actors, or after each scene is finished allow the rest of the class to say what they might have done had they been in the situation portrayed. To shorten the time this exercise takes, choose just one or two of the scenes to use. After each scene, encourage wild applause from the rest of the class.

If you have time, ask for comments from the class about what the actors playing themselves did well or could have done better. Don't worry if you don't have time for this, though; whether you get to talk about it in class or not, seeing these scenes played out will get your students to thinking how they would behave in such a situation.

Live It (5 min.)

To close this lesson, say something like: Leaders and people in authority who attack Christianity might do so because they fear it. Humans typically attack what they fear. Authority figures who want to be in charge of everything don't want anybody – including God – to be in charge of anything. It's our right as human beings, and our duty as Christians, to stand up against unfair attacks on our faith.

Then ask someone to close the lesson with prayer by saying something like: *Who feels led to pray, asking God to give us the strength, faith, and courage to stand up for our faith?*

Resources used: abcnews.go.com, cbc.ca, christianpost.com, foxnews.com, myfoxorlando.com, Seven Words of Men Around the Cross by Paul Moore, Theological Dictionary of the New Testament, telegraph.co.uk, Understanding the Mysteries of Human Behavior by Mark Leary, wmctv.com

© 2014 Discipleship Ministry Team of the Ministry Council of the Cumberland Presbyterian Church. All Rights Reserved.

Notes:

Real News or Not?

#1 On a Saturday morning in Raleigh, North Carolina, a church group went to a public park to distribute sausage biscuits and cups of coffee to homeless persons, just as they'd been doing for the past six years. This time they were met by police officers who told them distributing food in a public park was illegal without a permit. The officers said they would arrest anyone who gave food to the seventy homeless persons already gathered. The appropriate permit costs $800 per day.

#2 At a terrorism preparedness training event for Army reserves in Pennsylvania, an instructor for the US Army presented a list of religious extremist groups who pose a potential terrorist threat. Some of the groups on the list were the Ku Klux Klan, Al Qaeda, and evangelical Christians.

#3 A public school teacher in the UK specialized in teaching home-bound children. At one student's home, the teacher asked if she could pray for the sick student. The student said her family wasn't religious so the teacher did not pray. The teacher's boss, however, said this was bullying and fired the teacher.

#4 A twelfth-grader in Nova Scotia, Canada, was suspended for five days because he refused to stop wearing a Christian-themed shirt to school. His shirt said "Life is wasted without Jesus."

#5 When city officials in Memphis, Tennessee, learned that several churches had joined forces -- each church agreeing to house and feed twelve homeless persons one night a week during the winter months -- the officials said this violated a city ordinance that required an organization to have at least five acres of land before it could house persons overnight. The churches received citations and fines.

#6 A Brooklyn, New York, elementary teacher prayed in her classroom before school, after school, and in between classes, but never with students present. A new principal made fun of her faith and told her to stop this. When she did not stop, a false accusation of her touching a student caused her to be fired.

#7 Without allowing citizens to vote on the issue, city officials in Steubenville, Ohio changed the city's logo -- a stylized skyline featuring several of the city's prominent buildings -- because a cross was included, and they feared a lawsuit from an anti-Christian group. One of the city's largest employers is a Christian university; it's their chapel's cross that appeared in the logo.

#8 A middle school wrestling coach in Buncombe County, North Carolina, was reprimanded for wearing a Christian-themed shirt. School officials then instructed all employees to wear religion-neutral clothing.

#9 School officials in Cocoa, Florida, made a Christian eighth-grade girl change out of her pro-abstinence shirt that said, "Don't drink and park... accidents cause kids." The student was given another shirt to wear instead— the usual shirt used in cases of inappropriate attire. It read, "Tomorrow I will dress for success."

#10 In North Korea it is illegal to be Christian. Owning a Bible is grounds for execution. The government tells teachers to encourage children to report their Christian parents, who are then arrested and put in concentration camps or executed.

Improv Theatre
Handout A

Improv Theatre Scene Setup #1A
You are the manager of a fast food restaurant: Burger Bucket. You begin this scene by telling a new employee to stop wearing a cross necklace to work, even if it's worn under a shirt, because it might offend some customers. You will also tell him/her that he/she needs to stop talking about God, Jesus, the Bible, as well as going to church and youth group activities because these things might offend customers.

Improv Theatre Scene Setup #2A
You are the coach of a middle school synchronized swimming team. You've quietly made sure the team does not pray before or after practices and competitions because you think only weak people need religion, and you want your team to be strong. In this scene, your team is just about to hit the pool for your big competition against your toughest rivals: The Orange County Otters.

Improv Theatre Scene Setup #3A
You are a college professor who thinks that religion, especially Christianity, is just a bunch of made-up nonsense believed only by simple-minded people who can't think for themselves. God did not create the world. In fact, there obviously is no God because there is no proof of God. The Bible is complete fiction. If there ever was a man named Jesus, he was not divine but rather most likely insane. The only things Christianity has contributed to world history are wars, hatred, and anti-science stupidity. It's the first day of class. You begin this scene by announcing that any student who mentions Jesus or God will get an "F."

Improv Theatre
Handout B

Improv Theatre Scene Setup #1B
You just got a job at The Burger Bucket, working after school. Your boss, the manager, asks to speak to you just before your shift starts.

Improv Theatre Scene Setup #2B
You are on the middle school synchronized swimming team. Your team is just about to hit the pool for your big competition against your toughest rivals: The Orange County Otters. You begin this scene by asking the coach if the team can pray together before the competition.

Improv Theatre Scene Setup #3B
You are you, a few years from now. It's the first day of a new semester at college. You're sitting in the classroom of a professor you've never had before.

I'm Thirsty
by Jeff Ingram

Scripture: John 19:28-30

Theme: What do we mean by thirst, and why was Jesus thirsty on the cross?

Resource List

- Grape juice
- White distilled vinegar
- Tasting cups (small, 4-8oz cups)
- Water
- Container (large bowl or dish)
- Newsprint or white board
- Small slips of paper, pencils or pens
- Tables for the tasting
- Room for exercising
- Optional: A clean sponge

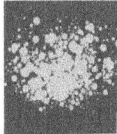 Leader Prep

- Before students arrive, mix a tiny amount of vinegar (approx. 1 oz) to some grape juice in your tasting cups. Use a 3:1 ratio of grape juice to vinegar. So, if you are doing 4 oz total, it will be 3 oz grape juice and 1 oz vinegar. Scale up or down, depending on how much you need in each cup. You shouldn't need a lot; this is just a taste.
- Have a bowl or other container ready for students to spit out their tastings. This is meant to simulate sour wine. They will not want to swallow this mixture. If someone does, it isn't harmful as they are both food grade ingredients, but it will taste pretty awful. You should encourage them to spit it out into a container after tasting.
- Have water readily available for students to drink after they have done the tasting. This will be very important as most will want something to drink after the tasting.
- Have enough slips of paper for each student to write down answers to each question.
- Read Psalm 69:21

Notes:

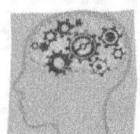

Leader Insight

Connecting to Your Students

Every day we experience thirst. Sometimes we thirst for something to drink; sometimes we thirst for something else. Thirst is defined as a desire to drink, but it is also defined as an insistent desire or a craving. In this lesson, we are exploring Jesus statement from the cross, "I'm thirsty."

We all thirst for something. You may understand your thirst. You may not. But each of your students is thirsting for something. When thinking about, and talking about, this subject with your group, connect with their thirst. They may not declare their thirst to you. Part of what you do as an accompanist on their journey may not be to satisfy their thirst, but to rather help them understand what their thirst is. Use this time to explore those feelings and see how you can connect their thirst to the thirst of Jesus.

Explaining the Bible

In John 19:28-30, we are in the last stages of Jesus' time on the cross. It appears that Jesus is asking for a drink because he is thirsty. Or is he?

No doubt Jesus experienced extreme thirst while being crucified. He would have lost a substantial quantity of bodily fluid, both blood and sweat, through what he had endured even prior to crucifixion. Thus his statement, "I am thirsty" was, on the most obvious level, a request for something to drink. In response the soldiers gave Jesus "sour wine" (v. 29), a cheap beverage common among lower-class people in the time of Jesus.

There is an interesting insert here. It says that he was fulfilling the prophecy by asking for a drink. In Psalm 69:20-21, David is giving a prophecy about the one who will be the savior. This prophecy indicates that the savior would announce his thirst, and they would give him vinegar to drink. When Jesus announces his thirst on the cross, all they had was sour wine, or vinegar. The vinegar was placed on a sponge and Jesus drink from it. When he drank it, he was not satisfied in his thirst, but he was satisfied in fulfilling the prophecy from David. In other words, the purpose of Christ's words, "I am thirsty" was to fulfill the Scripture. Though there is no specific reference in the text of the Gospel, it's likely that John was thinking of Psalm 69, which includes this passage:

> Their insults have broken my heart,
> and I am in despair.
> If only one person would show some pity;
> if only one would turn and comfort me.
> But instead, they give me poison for food;
> they offer me sour wine for my thirst.
> (vv. 20-21)

It is important to note that Jesus was a scholar of the religious texts and would know this prophecy from David's Psalm. In fact, Jesus fulfilled 28 prophecies from David and other prophets during his crucifixion. This was the last one before he died. He said, "I am thirsty," and they gave him the sour wine. And finally he said, "It is fulfilled." His last act before dying made the prophecy complete.

As he suffered, Jesus embodied the pain of the people of Israel—suffering that had been recorded in the Psalms. Jesus was suffering for the sin of Israel, even as he was taking upon himself the sin of the world.

This could have confused people. Throughout the Gospel of John, Jesus provided abundantly for those who were hungry and thirsty. Jesus not only provided for the physical needs of those who came to him, but he also offered them spiritual nourishment—nourishment that would not go away or need to be replenished.

Those hearing Jesus' words would remember the time that Jesus met the Samaritan woman at the well and offered her living water. They would remember Jesus' feeding of the multitudes. Jesus told them that the food wasn't why they should follow him—they should follow him because he was the true Bread of Life. Those hearing John's gospel would also remember Jesus' words during the Festival of Booths inviting all who thirst to come to him and drink of him (experience and believe) so that they would be filled with the living water. (Veen)

Theological Underpinnings

This utterance of, "I am thirsty" can also be viewed as a last yearning of Jesus. He thirsted in his most trying of times. We all thirst, but when do we declare that we are thirsty? If we are thirsty, we just grab a drink and our thirst is satiated. We never really say it, unless we are desperate. Only when we need someone to help us (or we just want to complain), do

Notes:

we declare our thirst. When we declare this thirst to others, we are asking for help or letting people know that we need to satisfy our thirst.

Jesus did not die until he knew that he could fulfill what he was here on earth to do: to teach, preach, and help us understand the fulfillment of God's Kingdom here on earth. There is a confidence that is displayed by Jesus in John's description of the crucifixion. Jesus is portrayed as always being in control of what is happening along with his thoughts and emotions, despite the horrific things that are happening to him. Keep in mind what he has gone through till this point. He has been whipped, beaten, carried a heavy cross, and been mocked mercilessly the entire time. To be able withstand this, and then carry on until he knows his mission is accomplished, is incredible. Jesus knows that he is fulfilling a prophecy while going through an unimaginable circumstance.

This puts all of our suffering into a unique perspective. While we know that we are accomplishing some sort of purpose, we often get beaten down by our circumstances. While Jesus' suffering is much more literal than ours, we still have these times where it feels like we are taking on the world, and we lose our perspective. It is encouraging and empowering to think that despite all he went through, Jesus was able to keep his perspective about what his ministry is. The hope is that we can identify our own suffering and crosses during ministry by looking at Jesus' example.

Applying the Lesson to Your Own Life

How do you respond to Jesus' statement, "I am thirsty"? What does this statement suggest to you about Jesus? About yourself?

In reflecting on Jesus' statement, "I am thirsty," think of your own thirst. It's nothing like that of Jesus. What does it mean to be thirsty for Jesus?

Rejoice in the fact that he suffered physical thirst on the cross – and so much more – so that your thirst for the water of life might be quenched.

Go beyond the boundaries of the thirst that you experience when you need a drink. Explore the thirst of our souls and our spirits. This is the thirst that drives us and makes us who we are. It is the embodiment of our goals and ambitions. Explore this in yourselves and in your students.

The Lesson

Get Started (15 min.)

Welcome everyone into the group, and then immediately get them into some kind of exercise. If you have room, have them run sprints, do jumping jacks, push-ups, or sit-ups; do this indoors or outside. The point here is to get them tired and a little sweaty. Don't overdo it, but at least get them breathing hard.

After you have done this, pass out pencils and the small slips of paper and direct them to the tables you have set up with the grape juice.

Say: *In John 19:28-30, Jesus is on the cross and says that he is thirsty. Thirst is one of our most basic desires and something that we experience daily. When we are thirsty, we can find some sort of beverage and generally be satisfied. When Jesus announced his thirst from the cross, only sour wine was made available to him. The wine was soaked into a sponge and lifted towards his mouth. He took a drink. Imagine what that might have been like. (Pause for a couple seconds.) To see what this is like, you have before you a tasting cup of our own "Sour Wine." This is vinegar and grape juice. You also have a bowl at your table for you to spit out what you have tasted. Don't worry if you accidentally swallow—it won't harm you. There is some water that you will need to drink after you spit out your tasting, but wait for instruction before you drink your water.*

Have everyone take their sample, and pay attention to the reactions of the students as they taste.

After they taste, have them write down their initial reaction to the taste of the "sour wine" on the slip of paper that you gave them. Ask them to put their initial reaction into a bowl or container you have made available.

After you bring everyone back to the main group, give them the instruction to drink their water.

Once everyone has some water, have them write down their initial reaction to drinking the water after such a long time.

Ask them to hold on to this piece of paper.

Notes:

Notes:

Take two or three reactions from the bowl and read them out loud to the group.

Break the group into smaller groups of 2-4 students. If your group is not big enough, feel free to discuss this with the whole group.

Discussion Questions:
- What was your reaction to the "Sour Wine"?
- What was it like when you tasted the water after the wine?

Listen Up (20 min.)

Discussion Question:
- What do you think it means to thirst?

Have someone read John 19:28-30.

Say: *We're going to look at three areas of this passage.*
1. *Jesus was thirsty.*
2. *Jesus knew ¬that the scriptures would be fulfilled.*
3. *Jesus had completed his ministry on earth.*

The most literal way to interpret verse 28 is that Jesus was thirsty! In the literal sense, thirst comes about when you haven't had anything to drink for a period of time. Generally, when you start to get dehydrated, you have headaches, feel weak, and tired. You have probably experienced this before after a lot of physical activity or just a long period of time without drinking anything. Jesus went through a lot even before being crucified. He was beaten, whipped and carried a cross a long distance. When Jesus asked for something to drink, he had been on the cross for a long period of time. After all of this, Jesus' literal thirst is great. This can be one reason why Jesus made the statement "I am thirsty." Thirst is a basic instinct for all living things.

- Why does John include this detail of Jesus being thirsty?
- What does this have to do with the overall story of Jesus' death?

Have someone read Psalm 69:20-21.

When it came to his ministry, Jesus' drink was one of the last objectives of a bigger goal of redemption. And as always, his mind was steeped in Scripture. In John, Jesus is quoting Psalm 69: 21, "for my thirst they gave me vinegar to drink." Throughout his sufferings, Jesus' mind was centered upon God's Word and its fulfillment.

Jesus knew that the scriptures would be fulfilled. He was sent to earth to fulfil the prophecies proclaimed in the Old Testament, including those found in Psalms. Jesus is fully in control of all that happens on the day of his crucifixion. Jesus always sees the larger picture while he is going through this day. The simple fact that he could remember and make that statement while going through unimaginable torture shows that he knew the moment was bigger than just a Roman execution; this was something bigger than the literal thirst he may have been feeling at that moment.

Discussion Question:
- Do you think he was remembering this prophecy, or was he just describing a literal thirst? Why?

Jesus knew he was on earth for a purpose. Part of that was to spread the word of God and the light of the world, ultimately bringing us all into that light. Jesus knew that for his ministry to be complete, he had to die. He was here to show us the light of God and provide the living waters for all of us. He knew that thirst is a desire we all have; it was a desire of his and a requirement of his ministry. When he became thirsty for the living waters that God provided, he knew that he was providing the water for us all and his ministry was complete.

Discussion Questions:
- What do you think of Jesus' certainty about his ministry?
- Is it reassuring to you to know that Jesus is that certain about his ministry? Why or why not?

Notes:

Notes:

Now What? (10 min.)

What is the living water?

Have someone read John 7:37-38.

Jesus says that whoever is thirsty should come and drink from the living waters that he provides. (John 7:37-38) In this section, you will break your group into smaller groups to have a discussion about what exactly is living water. Pose the following questions to your group, and have them come up with, and write down, one or two word answers to the questions as a group. Give them two minutes to come up with their one word answer.

You can give them an opportunity to expand on their answers individually.
- Earlier you experienced a literal thirst after going through the exercises. What did that experience feel like?
- What was it like to have a drink of water?
- What is Jesus referring to when speaks of living water (the story of the woman at the well)?
- How do the living waters refresh you?

Live It (10 min.)

Have someone read John 19:28-30 again.

Close with a prayer in a circle, and pray for the relief of thirst for themselves, their community, and the world.

Give each student a dixie cup and let them draw water from a ceramic pot labelled "Living Water."

Before everyone drinks, say together:

> *Jesus, I am thirsty.*
> *Please come and fill me.*
> *Earthly things have left me dry.*
> *Only you can satisfy.*
> *All I want is more of you.*
> *Amen.*

Resources used: http://www.leslieveen.com/, Feasting on the Word Year B, Volume 2 John 18:1-19:42 (Bartlett and Taylor)

© 2014 Discipleship Ministry Team of the Ministry Council of the Cumberland Presbyterian Church. All Rights Reserved.

Notes:

Crucifixion
by Andy McClung

Scripture: Matthew 27:33-35, Mark 15:22-25, Luke 23:33, John 19:16-18

Theme: Jesus' crucifixion, while a terrible way to die, was nothing out of the ordinary... except for the startling conclusion and its implications for all humankind!

Resource List

- Cheap pocket crosses
- One large nail, about 4 or 5 inches long
- Many nails, 1 to 2 inches long, with small heads
- A few hammers
- A rectangle of ½ inch or thicker plywood (at least 2 feet by 3 feet)
- A few spools of brightly colored string (various colors)
- A few pairs of scissors
- Mid-sized cross
- "Ten Ways to Die" cards
- (Optional) A chin-up bar that fits over a doorframe

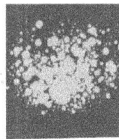

Leader Prep

- With a pencil, lightly outline a cross on the plywood.

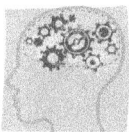

Leader Insight

Connecting to Your Students
If your students have grown up in church, they've heard about Jesus' crucifixion many times. They may have been to youth rallies where they heard a sermon about how much Jesus suffered on the cross for them— a sermon delivered in such a way as to elicit strong emotions. They may have seen filmed depictions of the crucifixion— some sanitized and some graphic. If your students have not grown up in church, they have probably seen or heard several depictions of the crucifixion anyway. They may be bored of the topic.

This lesson isn't an attempt to gross out anybody, make anybody feel guilty for Jesus' actions on their behalf, or rehash well-known information. Instead, it offers a fresh look at something central to our faith, encourages students to ask questions, and demonstrates that the crucifixion of Jesus is an example of God taking something quite common and making it sacred.

Leader Tip:
The word "crucifixion" comes from Latin "cruci figo" which means "I fasten to a cross."

Leader Tip:
The vertical piece of a cross is called a "stipe," and the horizontal piece is called a "patibulum."

Explaining the Bible

By the time Jesus was walking around, crucifixion was already at least a thousand years old. Historians note that the first crucifixions involved the impaling of a person on a sharp stake and then hoisting them off the ground as a message to one's enemies. You can imagine how demoralizing it must have been to see your friends dying in slow agony, hanging from a stake outside your enemy's fortress while birds and animals picked away at their flesh. Various rulers over the centuries used crucifixion this way, sometimes crucifying thousands of their enemies at once.

The Roman Empire started taking over other kingdoms around the Mediterranean Sea about 200 years before Jesus was born. About thirty years before Jesus was born, the Romans had taken over Jesus' homeland. They couldn't keep an adequate number of soldiers in every place they'd conquered, so there was constant concern over defeated locals rising up against their empire. Rome appointed governors to each region, and these governors used crucifixion to keep the locals in line. Anybody from the conquered lands found guilty of stirring up rebellion against Rome was crucified; the crucifixion acted as both punishment and deterrent from further rebellions.

Roman crucifixion was reserved for enemies of the state. Crimes against people were punished in other ways. So the two men crucified near Jesus were indeed criminals – at least according to Roman law – but it's unlikely they were thieves. During Jesus' lifetime there were probably hundreds of crucifixions performed around Jerusalem, and dozens of those crucified were men claiming to be the messiah trying to raise an army to get rid of the Romans. Jesus was probably quite familiar with crucifixion. He may have even seen crucified bodies when he went to Jerusalem at the age of twelve (Luke 2:41-42).

The Romans performed so many crucifixions they had to refine it to make it more practical. Instead of using only a single, upright stake that had to be raised and fixed in place for each victim, they began attaching the victim to a shorter piece of wood (patibulum) that would be hoisted up and attached to an upright, permanently fixed stake (stipe). This also enabled further humiliation of the victim by parading them through town with the patibulum on their shoulders. They used two kinds of crosses: the "tau cross" which is shaped like a capital "T", and the "Latin cross," which is shaped like a lower-case "t". Because a sign was put on the cross above Jesus's head (Matthew 27:37, Luke 23:38), it is commonly believed that Jesus was crucified on a Latin cross.

A person crucified by the Roman Empire in the First Century began suffering long before he made it to the cross. First, he was stripped, tied to a post, and hit on his shoulders, back, and legs more than thirty times with a leather whip with several "tails" into which were woven lead weights and sharp bits of bone. One witness to such a flogging wrote that veins were laid bare; muscles, tendons, and bowels were exposed. The blood loss would have been great. The victim was probably in serious to critical condition after the flogging, which may explain why Jesus needed help carrying his cross.

Why whip or flog somebody who's about to be killed anyway? For intimidation. A beaten and bloody body hanging from a cross makes a stronger statement than a clean and uninjured body.

Next, the victim's hands were nailed or tied to a patibulum, and he was forced to carry it as far as a mile along the Via Dolorosa, or the "Way of Sorrow." If he fell, he likely would land on his chest with the weight of the patibulum crashing down on his back. It's likely that the Roman soldiers made a show of this walk, and some people in the streets hurled insults and other things at the victim as he passed.

Why do the gospels have no details of the crucifixion? Because when they were written everybody knew exactly what crucifixion involved. They had seen it for themselves.

The people who witnessed Jesus' crucifixion had seen dozens or more. The cross that Jesus hung from was no different than the one to his right or left, nor the dozens more dotting the landscape. Some had dying people on them; some had dead bodies on them.

Theological Underpinnings

When we think of Jesus being arrested, put on trial, and crucified, we may tend to think these were big events; that the world stood still while they happened; that the people involved knew something big was happening; that everybody was holding their breath to see how things would turn out. We tend to think this because these events are important to us, and we know that they were leading up to one of the most important moments in history: Jesus' resurrection.

It's likely, though, that all these things seemed very common

Leader Tip:

There are no 2,000-year-old instruction manuals on how to do a crucifixion. What we know is based on research, archeology, and logical guesses.

Notes:

to the people who were involved in them because such things were very common in first century Judea; Floggings and crucifixions were carried out all the time.

This takes nothing away from the humiliation and pain that Jesus suffered during his crucifixion. Instead, it reminds us that God, in Jesus, experienced everything we experience yet remained sinless— even to the point of forgiving those torturing and murdering him! The commonness of Jesus' crucifixion also reminds us that God takes common, ordinary, not-special things and makes them sacred. That's what God does with common, ordinary, sinful people who entrust their lives to him through Jesus.

We may wonder why Jesus had to go through the horror of crucifixion, or if Jesus really had to die so horribly to save us. Different Christians – even different Cumberland Presbyterians – have many different answers to this question, like "Jesus died to pay the price for our sins," or "Jesus died to show us how we should respond to violence and injustice." What all Cumberland Presbyterians agree on, though, is that by choosing to die on the cross, Jesus fulfilled God's plan to offer us a way to be saved from our sin and obtain eternal life (Confession of Faith 3.07, 3.09).

Applying the Lesson to Your Own Life
Close your eyes and imagine the events before and during Jesus' crucifixion. (Go ahead, take a moment.) Most of those images did not come from scripture. Why do you think the Bible has so few details about the crucifixion itself?

What do you think about Roman Catholics who use a crucifix, while we Protestants use an empty cross? The crucifix affirms that Jesus can empathize with us in our suffering. What does the empty cross affirm?

Recall a time that you suffered great physical pain. Now recall a time that you suffered public humiliation. Which was worse? If those two occurrences had been combined, could you have withstood the suffering?

For you, does the crucifixion "rank" higher, lower, or equal in importance compared to the other parts of the whole Christ event – the incarnation, birth, life, death, resurrection, and ascension of Jesus? Does your practice of your faith reflect this ranking?

The Lesson

Get Started (10 min.)

Before class, prepare ten sheets of paper with the following "Ways to Die" printed on them, one per sheet. These are going to get handled a lot, so consider using heavy paper. Shuffle the cards, or randomly spread them out on a table just before starting this exercise.
- Burning to death in a fire
- Drowning
- Falling from a great height
- Being mauled to death by an animal
- Freezing to death
- Bleeding to death
- Suddenly, in an explosion
- Starving to death / dying of thirst
- Captured and tortured to death by bad guys
- Executed as a criminal with reporters and cameras present

Have a student rank the cards with what he or she considers the absolute worst way to die at the top and the easiest ways to die on the bottom. Put the cards on a bulletin board with pushpins, a wall with masking tape, or just have the student lay the cards out on the floor. When the first student is done, ask one or more of the questions below, and then have another student rearrange the cards according to his or her personal ranking. Then ask that student one or more of the questions below. Unless you have a huge class, continue until all students have had a turn.

You will need to customize the questions according to how each student has ranked the cards. Mix it up: try not to ask the same questions about the same ways to die.

Discussion Questions:
- Why do you think [a high card] would be worse than [a low card]?
- What if [a low card] were to happen in front of a crowd of strangers? Would that move it higher?
- Why is [low card] not as bad as [high card]?
- What would be the worst part of [high card]?
- Would [any card] be better or worse if your friends and family were watching it happen?

Notes:

Notes:

Leader Tip:
Be prepared for questions or comments about death or dying. You may pursue these tangent paths or choose to refocus on the original lesson.

Leader Tip:
OPTIONS: Use a portable chin-up bar that fits over the door frame; a swing set or monkey bars outside; ask a clever craftsman to build something temporary in the room just for this lesson; or you could ask a male student where the boys do chin-ups in the building.

After each student has had a turn, or time is running out, ask this general question of the whole class: What do you think would be the best way to die? Allow a minute for them to think, if needed, and then allow anyone to respond. Also allow explanations of responses.

Unless your students are very unusual, you should be able to transition into the lesson by saying something like: *This class agrees with the people of every civilization for at least the last 3,000 years — crucifixion is one of the worst ways to die. It involves public humiliation, prolonged suffering, and lots of pain. Today we're going to explore just what was involved in Roman crucifixion, which is how Jesus died.*

Listen Up (20 min.)

Set up the chin-up bar and have students take turns — as you continue the lesson — hanging by their hands as long as possible, with their hands as wide apart as possible, and feet off the ground. Set the rules: when one student comes off the bar another gets on it; everybody will get a turn. This will be a distraction during the lesson, but the hands-on learning will be worth it.

Bring out the cross. It needs to be bigger than jewelry but smaller than life-sized. It can be fancy and pretty, or simple and rugged. A free-standing cross from the sanctuary would do nicely. Simply place this cross somewhere prominent in the room without comment and leave it there throughout the lesson.

Discussion Question:
- What's the grossest, bloodiest thing you've ever seen—either in a movie or in real life? (Allow brief responses, then state:) Crucifixion was worse.

Share some of the information about the history of crucifixion from the information above.

Discussion Question:
- What's the worst pain you've ever felt? How long did it last?

Allow brief responses, then say: *Crucifixion was worse.*

Share some of the following information about crucifixion. As you speak, have students pass around the large nail.

The victim of crucifixion, after having been whipped and marched through the streets carrying his patibulum, was hoisted up onto the stipe and the patibulum was fixed to the stipe. He hung there, in public, completely naked.

It's unknown if all victims' hands were nailed to the patibulum. Some may have been tied. We know Jesus was nailed because of the nail wounds mentioned in John 20. If the hands were nailed through the palms, they would also have been tied at the wrist because a nail through the palm can only support forty pounds before the nail rips through the flesh and tendons. Since the Greek word for "hand" can also mean "hand and wrist," it's possible that the nails were driven through the bones of the wrist to support more weight, or just farther up the arm between the two bones of the forearm.

The feet were also nailed to the cross, either sideways through the heel and into the sides of the stipe, or with the feet placed on top of each other and one nail driven through both feet. Roman crosses probably did not have the little footrests seen in artwork.

Crucifixion could lead to death several different ways. The human body can only take so much trauma before shutting down. As it included dehydration, exhaustion, exposure, contusions, abrasions, blunt force wounds, possible shoulder dislocations, and puncture wounds, crucifixion was plenty traumatic.

When the human body loses a large volume of blood the heart beats faster trying to move the remaining blood throughout the body. When so much blood is lost that the heart can't keep up, the body goes into hypovolemic shock. This leads to death. The wounds of crucifixion victims were never bandaged, and the wounds to their backs remained open because they were scraped against the cross with every breath.

Hanging by the arms strains the chest muscles to the point

Notes:

Notes:

where the victim can only inhale, unless he pushes up with his nailed feet to relieve the strain on his chest, therefore scraping his flogged back up and down the wooden stipe each time. It was easier to do this with nails driven sideways through the heels than with one nail driven through the tops of both feet. Eventually the victim would become too tired to push himself up anymore, carbon dioxide would build up in his lungs, he would become hypoxic (too little oxygen in the blood), and he would asphyxiate. If the Roman soldiers needed to hasten death, they would break the bones in the victim's lower legs, making him unable to push up to exhale anymore.

There are accounts of persons taking many hours, even days, to die from crucifixion. Nine days is the longest mentioned in ancient texts. It took only about six hours for Jesus to die on the cross.

It may be that he fell while carrying his patibulum; scripture doesn't say, but there had to be some reason the guards grabbed Simon to help. Such a fall could have bruised his heart. A bruised heart working overtime would develop an aneurysm. If that heart continued to work overtime, the aneurysm would rupture, letting blood into the pericardium (the sack of clear fluid that surrounds the heart), filling it, and stretching it tight. A spear stabbed into the body could easily puncture the pericardium and release blood and a clear liquid that looked like water. Support for this theory includes the facts that Jesus could speak, which is difficult for someone asphyxiating, and it seems he was conscious right up to his death, while hypovolemia causes one to pass out.

Rome used crucifixion against Jews and Christians for another 300 years until Emperor Constantine became a Christian after a supernatural vision… of a cross! Crucifixions still happen today in places like Darfur and Saudi Arabia.

Now What? (15 min.)

Before class use a pencil to lightly outline a cross on the rectangle of plywood. Make your drawn cross no more than three inches wide at any point. It shouldn't be perfect; don't use a ruler.

Have students take turns nailing the 1 to 2 inch nails into the wood, following your pencil marks to roughly make the shape of a cross. Make sure they only drive the nails in deep enough for them to be sturdily in the wood. Use lots and lots of nails. The end result should be ugly: crowded, no straight lines, nails at different depths and angels, cold metal against rough wood.

Hold up the finished product for all to see. Point out that it's not very pretty and that's it's just a bunch of common, every-day items from the hardware store.

Assign some students to start cutting the colorful string into various lengths, ranging from three to twelve inches. Assign other students to take those bits of string and weave them around and inbetween the nails. Use lots and lots of string. At some point have the students swap tasks so everybody gets a chance to both cut and weave.

As students work, read aloud either Matthew 27:33-35, Mark 15:22-25, Luke 23:33, John 19:16-18, or all four.

If you have a large class, make two or more crosses this way.

When time is up, hold up the new cross for all to see.

Say: *Two thousand years ago God took an ugly cross, a common thing used for torture, a symbol of fear and intimidation, and changed it into a symbol of hope and love. We just took a piece of lumber, some nails, and some string – all common, not-special things— and made them into a thing of beauty, a symbol of hope and love.*

Consider placing the cross where the whole congregation can see it.

Just in Case:

If a student asks whether or not ancient Jews practiced crucifixion themselves, you can say, "No." Judaic Law, given by God to Moses, may seem to promote crucifixion in Deuteronomy 21:22-23. While the Law does allow for capital punishment, this passage does not promote the horrible torture of crucifixion, but rather allows for a public display of the offender's body after execution to discourage others from committing similar offenses. This posthumous punishment was reserved only for idolaters and blasphemers.

DIGGING DEEPER

Archeological evidence of crucifixions is extremely rare because wood, rope, and flesh decay; iron nails were removed and reused; and the bodies of most crucifixion victims were not buried but just tossed aside— their flesh eaten and bones scattered by wild animals. That's why an accidental discovery in 1968, was so valuable to archeologists. The ossuary (a stone coffin) of a man named Jehohanan who was crucified sometime in the first century was found by construction workers. Archeologists were allowed to study his skeleton and ossuary, as well as take pictures and measurements before the whole thing was reburied. Jehohanan still had a 4 ½ inch nail stuck through his right heel, passing through from left to right. He must have been from a wealthy or well-connected family to have received a proper burial after crucifixion. Jesus only received a proper burial because the wealthy Joseph of Arimathea interceded for him.

Live It (5 min.)

Give each student a pocket-cross to take home, carry with him or her, or give away to someone else. Say something like: God took an ordinary cross and made it sacred. When we entrust our lives to God through Jesus, God makes ordinary us, sacred.

Resources used: The Case for Christ by Lee Strobel, "Crucifixion" by the History Channel, The New Bible Dictionary

© 2014 Discipleship Ministry Team of the Ministry Council of the Cumberland Presbyterian Church. All Rights Reserved.

Wait, Let's See
by Jeff Ingram

Scripture: Matthew 27:49 and Mark 15:36

Theme: Even though Jesus was mocked throughout his trial and crucifixion, God was still with him. Even though he was mocked for asking to be saved, God was with him. When mankind abandoned Jesus, God was still with him.

Resource List

- Music player (laptop, iPod, MP3 player, CD player, speakers, etc.)
- Song: "Save Me," by Muse.
- Lyrics to "Save Me," by Muse displayed.
- White board or newsprint for posting questions
- Markers
- Pens
- Paper

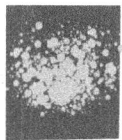

Leader Prep

- Write questions on newsprint or whiteboard so that the small groups can refer to the questions as they discuss
- Read Matthew 27, Mark 15, and Psalm 22. These passages will help you understand the events surrounding the crucifixion and give context to the prophecy Jesus fulfills.
- Song: "Save Me," by Muse. Can be found on iTunes, Spotify (http://open.spotify.com/track/3MbkURW6xUuXYMyZz08qDo), or YouTube (https://www.youtube.com/watch?v=zV8yLLphihk)

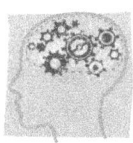

Leader Insight

Connecting to Your Students
The crucifixion story is something that all of your students have probably heard at one point or another. They probably know the story, but only in the context of what happened to Jesus. They know that he was crucified, and through that crucifixion he died for our sins. They are probably not as familiar with the crowd that was around Jesus as he was being crucified. It is rarely talked about, and most of the attention is on what physically happened to Jesus.

Notes:

The crowd was verbally abusive to Jesus as he was being led to the crucifixion site and as he was crucified. They denied him, mocked him, and were generally ruthless in what they did and said. This may be something that you and your students can relate to. We've all had those moments where it seems like everyone is against us. The crowd just keeps pouring on the hatred and never lets up. It is easy to think about those words that Jesus said: "My God, my God, why have you forsaken me?" During difficult times we may feel that God has left us, but God hasn't abandoned us. The people that are mocking us are the ones who have left us. God is with us during these times; it is the people that have abandoned us. And when those who are close to us abandon us, it is easy to lose sight of our God.

Explaining the Bible
In this passage, we are reading Jesus' final moments on the cross. He has already uttered the phrase "My God, My God, Why have you forsaken me?" at this point in the story. The crowd surrounding Jesus has been tormenting and mocking him through the entire crucifixion. They have put a crown of thorns on his head, they have stripped him, and they have called him the King of the Jews (facetiously). In Jesus' final moments, he cried out. He cried out to God, asking to be saved. The crowd heard this, and while some tried to help, others mocked him by saying, "let us see if Elijah will save him." (Matthew 27:49, Mark 15:36) They watched as Jesus cried out again and then breathed his last breath. (Matthew 27:50, Mark 15:37)

The story of Jesus' life ended with this final mocking. Jesus was brought into this world to suffer. Part of his suffering was the mocking and ridicule from the crowd. The crowd is unnamed in this telling of the Good Friday story and probably for good reason; it makes it easier identify with, and place ourselves in, the crowd. Keeping this crowd nameless and faceless, while referring to them only as "the crowd," allows us the opportunity to imagine who we would find watching Jesus on the cross. So often, our own faces can be found in the crowd in this story. We were the ones who were mocking, shunning, and turning away. The crowd was waiting to see if Elijah would come and save Jesus, rather than doing something about the crucifixion that was taking place in front of them.

So we ask this question: "Who really needed the saving on that day?" While the crowd insisted that Jesus needed saving from Elijah, it was really the crowd who needed to be saved by Jesus. Jesus knew his sacrifice. He knew what was before him. He also knows what is before us. So while the crowd may have thought that Jesus was the one in need of a savior, it turns out that it is us in that faceless, nameless crowd who needs saving.

Theological Underpinnings

In this passage, Jesus utters no words. He is just mocked. The statement prior to this is Jesus saying, "My God, My God, Why have you forsaken me?" This statement was part of a prophecy told of in the Psalms. David said this in Psalm 22. This was David's plea to be set free from suffering.

Jesus was stating this as a part of his fulfilment of the prophecy. When people heard it, they thought he was questioning God. They thought he was asking God to take him off the cross. With the weight of the world's sin on his shoulders and the unbearable physical pain of the cross, Jesus may have felt abandoned by God. He may have also felt completely abandoned by all of humanity.

What the crowd missed was that Jesus knew God would not abandon him in his most trying times, but Jesus knew that he would be abandoned by the people. If you continue reading in Psalm 22, you'll see that David is asking God why he was suffering while everybody mocked him. Jesus knew this was part of his fulfillment; that others would mock him as he cried out; that others would not understand his cries for salvation, not by God, but from the sins of those around him. He was not asking God to save him, but that through his suffering, the rest of us would be saved.

God demonstrates just how much we are loved through the suffering and mocking endured on the cross. We can be sure that God's grace and presence are always close by. This is what Jesus believed as he was dying.

Applying the Lesson to Your Own Life

Have you ever felt the need to be saved?

Have you ever just wanted to cry out and have someone save you?

Jesus felt this need when he was on the cross. He cried out and asked why God had forsaken him. He cried out in public in front of a crowd that had gathered to watch him get executed. They were questioning him and his authority. In response to his cries, they mocked him. They wanted to see

Notes:

God save him and take him off the cross. Sometimes, when we are in our darkest times, we ask for help. We ask to be saved, but all we hear are people telling us how weak we are. If we ask for help, we hear that we should be able to handle our own problems.

The Lesson

Get Started (15 min.)

As your group gathers, hand out pieces of paper and pens. When everyone is situated, ask them to:
- Write down an instance when you witnessed someone being mocked.
- Write how you thought the person being mocked felt.
- Write down an instance when you were being mocked.
- Write down how you felt when you were being mocked.

Give them 8-10 minutes to write down their responses. Ask them to be as detailed as they can be.

After everyone has had a chance to write down their responses, ask if anyone would like to share what they wrote. It can be either their personal experience, or something they have witnessed. Make it clear that no one has to share something they aren't comfortable sharing with the whole group. Be clear that this is not a time for gossip and to not use specific names. Don't force it, but encourage at least one response.

Listen Up (20 min.)

Break your group up into small groups of at least 4. If you have a small group, you can do this as one group.

Have someone read Matthew 27:49.

Have another student read Mark 15:36.

Without going any further into the context of where this verse falls in the story of Jesus' crucifiction, ask each group to discuss the following question for 5 minutes.

Discussion Question:
- What is going on in these passages?

Have someone read Matthew 27:27-31, and 27:45-50.

Have another student read Mark 15:16-20, and 15:33-38.

Allow 6-7 minutes to discuss the following questions in their small group.

Discussion Questions:
- Now that you have read this in context, have your thoughts about what is going on in these passages changed? Why or why not?
- What do you think the crowd of people is doing to Jesus?

Keep them in their groups, but engage all students in the large group discussion.

- How did your initial thoughts change after hearing the passage in context?

It becomes apparent that they were mocking Jesus' for calling out for help.

Discussion Questions:
- Have you ever been mocked for asking for help?
- Have you ever been mocked for your faith?

Notes:

Notes:

Now What? (10 min.)

Give everyone another slip of paper to write with. Remaining in the room, ask everyone to go and spend some time reflecting on this story. As they are reflecting on the story have them write down what they think Jesus felt as he was being mocked on the cross.

After giving them a couple of minutes to reflect, start playing the song, "Save Me" by Muse. While they are listening to the song, have them write down their thoughts about the song and how it relates to Jesus' calling out to be saved.

Display the lyrics to "Save Me."

Human Clay

Split your group into small groups of at least 4. If your group isn't that large, then you can do this with one group. Each group will come up with a sculpture that depicts the savaltion they saw in the song and in Jesus on the cross. Give them 5 minutes to construct their sculpture out of their group members.

Suggestion: Have each group come up with the sculpture, as well as one person acting as the artist to put it together. You could also just let them do this as a group. If you have students that display, or you hope would display more, leadership abilities, this is a good way to build those kinds of skills. The "artist" can then explain why they created what they did.

Live It (15 min.)

Bring everyone back to the group and form a circle.

In your own words, say the following:
Jesus was mocked as he was crucified. After calling out to God, he was mocked for calling out to God. Jesus was abandoned by the people around him. We all call out to God in our most trying moments, but we know that even though we may have been abandoned by people, God will never abandon us. God was with Jesus through his suffering and is with us through ours.

Close with a prayer of assurance that God will always be with us, even when people have abandoned us and mock us for asking to be saved.

© 2014 Discipleship Ministry Team of the Ministry Council of the Cumberland Presbyterian Church. All Rights Reserved.

Notes:

Notes:

Remember Me
by Mark Rackley

Scripture: Luke 23:32-43

Theme: We are sinners who are saved by the grace of God.

Resource List

- Bibles
- A few copies of the Confession of Faith of the Cumberland Presbyterian Church
- Newsprint or dry erase board
- Markers or dry erase markers
- A piece of paper and writing utensil for everyone in the class

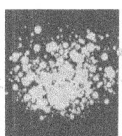

Leader Prep

- Be sure to read through each of the scriptures to familiarize yourself with each passage.
- Pray that the Holy Spirit would be working in each of your students during the week and lesson.

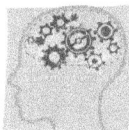

Leader Insight

Connecting to Your Students
The purpose of this lesson is to give students a chance to understand they're sinful people living in a sinful world, and God is waiting to save us through grace. This may be hard for young people who want to think of the world as a perfect place. Or for those young people that see the harsh realities of the world, they may resonate with a lesson focusing on the sinfulness of human nature. Either way, sin isn't an easy topic to discuss.

Explaining the Bible
Some people are oblivious to sin in their lives and in this world. They may not have faced the hard decisions where they must choose between the better of two evil choices. They may not have experienced the kind of failure in life that makes them question the goodness of life or their own worth.

Notes:

They may not have been hurt in one of their relationships to the point where mending takes more time than they can conceive.

Other people are in denial of sin. They don't want to talk about the bad parts of life. They simply want to focus on everything that is good and nice. They would rather not talk about the hurts, failures, and disappointments of life. They do not see any need to judge one's self or others by casting a grey cloud of failure and hurt over anyone.

Other people can't get away from sin. They like living the way they do. They are having fun without any concern for others. They couldn't care less about how their activities and lifestyle affect other people and the world around them. It is a dog-eat-dog world, and they are going to end up on top while having as much fun as possible along the way. It is all about them.

Other people are not worried about sin because they think that they are self-sufficient enough to overcome sin in their lives. They think that they can do enough good deeds to cancel out any bad deeds that they might do on purpose or unintentionally. They know what is expected of them, and they will do it. They know the rules of how to be a good person, and they will follow those rules, no matter what. As long as they do good, and have good intentions, they are alright.

Other people get so caught up in sin that they become stuck in guilt, shame, anger, fear, and/or distrust to the point that they have a hard time moving forward with their lives. This can also lead to struggles in relationships. Sometimes these people do not see themselves as worthy of relationships with others. At other times, these people are not able to forgive themselves or the people around them even for the smallest or simple offenses and failures. Other times they are too afraid to take the steps or make the changes involved in forgiveness. They are more comfortable with their present situation rather than what might happen if they do something different.

Many people who have left the church, or who have never been a part of the Body of Christ, say that they don't want be part of the church because Christians are so judgmental. They say Christians call people sinners and evil and are in need of saving. Even some Christians ask the question: "Why do we have to confess to be sinners." Why do we have to start our Christian walk with the realization that we are broken, imperfect, and sinful to our very core? Do we have to keep confessing our sins over and over again, or is once enough?

When we accept God's forgiveness for ourselves, we acknowledge that we are sinful rather than living in a state of denial. When we accept God's forgiveness for ourselves, we acknowledge that we cannot heal ourselves or make things right without God's help. When we accept God's forgiveness for ourselves, we put our faith in God that our relationship to the Father has been restored, and we can begin working on the relationships with the people who are in our lives.

When we join the church, we become a part of a group of people who understand and acknowledge we are broken and sinful. When we join the church, we become a part of a group of people who will help us to continue to grow in our relationship with God and with the people around us. We become a part of a group of people who know and believe that we do not have to put our faith in our accomplishments or achievements. Rather, we will put our faith in God who has a plan that includes us and who has the power to see that this plan is completed on time.

Theological Underpinnings
In this lesson we will hear and discuss what the Church says about sin from two different, but very similar, sources: the Bible and The Confession of Faith of the Cumberland Presbyterian Church. We will also take time to talk about different ways of dealing with sin. We will close our time together with a prayer where we will name some of our sins and then use the words of the criminal on the cross to approach God with reverence, relying on God's promise of forgiveness.

Please note that the discussion questions do not focus on how other people have sinned against us. Although we can acknowledge that we have been hurt by others and that we do not like how some people act or treat us, we are not attempting to focus on how others have wronged us or hurt us. Later lessons will address the hurt others have caused us, but we begin with a focus on our own wrong doings and God's grace.

Applying the Lesson to Your Own Life
Talking about sin can bring up some very painful experiences for everyone in the class. Please be mindful of what you already know about the people in your class so that old wounds will not simply be reopened and left to fester. Also,

Notes:

Notes:

if it becomes obvious that one or more of the people in the class need to talk one-on-one, please encourage them to talk with your pastor, an elder of your church, or someone else whom they trust and who is strong in their faith.

The Lesson

Get Started (15 min.)

Across the Spectrum

In this activity, the teacher makes a statement and the students stand in a spot in the room that represents where they are on a spectrum of "strongly agree", to "strongly disagree."

1. I find it easy to forgive other people.
2. I find it easy to ask for forgiveness from other people.
3. I find it easy to forgive myself.
4. I do not dwell on the things that people do that hurt me.
5. I do not dwell on the mistakes that I make.
6. People are inherently good.
7. People are inherently evil.
8. Most people want good things to happen to other people.
9. Most people are more worried about themselves than they are worried about others.
10. I like to be in control.
11. I would rather trust someone else to make decisions for me and take care of what needs to get done.
12. Most people are self-centered.
13. I push myself to do everything right.
14. I expect others to do their best at all times.
15. The church is a place where good people can gather together.
16. The church is a place for people who always do the right thing.

Discussion Question:
- Why do you have to confess to being a sinner and "repent" of your sin?

Most people would agree that they are not perfect, but they would also say they are not that bad either. In fact, most of us can probably list quite a few people that are a lot worse than we are: Hitler, Saddam Hussein, one of our siblings, a classmate or two, and maybe even someone who sits in the sanctuary with us during Sunday worship.

Discussion Question:
- If we all agree that we are not that bad (or as bad as some other people), when do we cross the line and become bad enough to be considered a bad person or a sinner?

The Bible describes us as sinners saved by the grace of God: "For it is by grace you have been saved, through faith - and this is not from yourselves, it is the gift of God— not by works, so that no one can boast. For we are God's workmanship, created in Christ Jesus to do good works, which God prepared in advance for us to do." (Ephesians 2:8-10)

You may have heard about Adam and Eve as described in Genesis 2:4-3:24. Adam and Eve did not handle temptation very well in that story. They did what God told them not to do. They listened to the advice of someone other than God. They ran from God after they sinned because they were afraid and ashamed. They blamed each other for what had happened. When they came under pressure in the presence of the truth of God, they went into the mode of self-preservation and became very self-centered. You can also read how their actions affected their relationship with each other, creation, and the God who created them. The story of Adam and Eve shows us that sin has been part of our story from the very beginning of time.

Discussion Questions:
- When have you acted like Adam and Eve?
- When have you done what God has told us not to do?
- When have you blamed someone else for the problems that you caused?
- When have you run from God (not literally)?
- When have you listened to the advice of the world, a friend, or someone you know, rather than the advice given in God's Word?

Notes:

Leader Tip:
For a creative visual presentation of this story, show students a clip from "The Bible" mini-series. This clip is from Episode 7 "Mission" and depicts the account of the disciples on the boat and seeing Jesus coming to them on the water. Help students understand this clip contains both Biblical information as well as added narrative, which is not in the Bible but is used to help tell the story.

Leader Tip:
It is easy to take these questions and apply them to other people. It is very easy for us to see the sin in the people around us, but the purpose of this lesson is to see the sin within ourselves.

- When have you listened to what the world says about your value, worth, and purpose, rather than what God says about us in the Bible?
- When have you been self-centered?
- When have you done whatever it took to maintain your status or personal well-being, even at the expense of other people?

Listen Up (15 min.)

Divide the class into small groups. Assign the following scripture passages to the groups and have them discuss how humans are described in them:
- Psalm 14:2-3
- Psalm 32:1-5
- Psalm 130
- Isaiah 6:1-7
- Romans 3:21-26
- Ephesians 2:1-10
- 1 John 1:8-10.

Discussion Questions:
- How is sin described in each of these scripture passages?
- What do these scripture passages say about us as individuals?
- What do these scripture passages say about us as a human race?

What do we as Cumberland Presbyterians say we believe about sin?
The Confession of Faith of the Cumberland Presbyterian Church was written and revised by the leaders of the Cumberland Presbyterian Church to be used as a witness to the Gospel.

"The purpose of a confession of faith is two-fold: 1) to provide a means whereby those who have been saved, redeemed, and reconciled by God through Jesus Christ in the power of the Holy Spirit understand and affirm their faith; and 2) to bear witness to God's saving activity in such a way that those who have not been saved, redeemed, and reconciled might believe in Jesus Christ as Lord and Savior and experience salvation. To this end a confession of faith is an affirmation of ancient truth in contemporary language." (Confession of Faith: for Cumberland Presbyterians August 2010, xv)

In that book, the leaders of the Cumberland Presbyterian Church read the Bible and then wrote what they felt was the Good News of what God was trying to say to us in God's Word. Look at what they wrote concerning sin as addressed in the Bible:

> 2.04 As did Adam and Eve, all persons rebel against God, lose the right relationship to God, and become slaves to sin and death. This condition becomes the source of all sinful attitudes and actions.
> 2.05 In willfully sinning all people become guilty before God and are under divine wrath and judgment, unless saved by God's grace through Jesus Christ.
> 2.06 The alienation of persons from God affects the rest of creation, so that the whole creation stands in need of God's redemption.

Discussion Questions:
- How does the quote from the Confession of Faith (2.04-2.06) compare to the scriptures that were mentioned earlier in this lesson?
- What other scripture references did the writers of the Confession of Faith use to inform what they wrote in 2.04-.206? (HINT: Look at the footnotes at the bottom of the page where this quote is found in the Confession of Faith.)
- What is the difference between a sinful attitude and a sinful action?
- How does our sinfulness affect our relationship with God?
- How does our sinfulness affect creation?

Notes:

Notes:

Leader Tip:
This list will be used in the closing prayer.

Now What? (20 min.)

What is the difference between an attitude and an action? Draw a line down the center of a piece of newsprint or a poster board so that we can make two lists, one on each side of the line. At the top of the paper, write "Attitudes" on one side of the line, and write "Actions" on the other side of the line. Have everyone in the class work together to create a list of different attitudes and actions that get in the way of our relationships with the people around us and our relationship with God.

Discussion Questions:
- How do the actions that we have listed affect our relationships with the people around us?
- How do the attitudes that we have listed affect our relationships with the people around us?
- How do the actions that we have listed affect our relationship with God?
- How do the attitudes that we have listed affect our relationship with God?
- How have our actions as individuals and as a human race affected the rest of creation in a way that causes creation to groan for God's presence and healing?

How do we deal with sin?

If we are honest with ourselves, we can admit that we are not perfect, and neither is this world. So if you are not perfect, how do you deal with your imperfection?

Listed below are four possible responses we might have to our own sinfulness:

1. We can deny our sinfulness. As we said earlier, we are not that bad. In fact, we look pretty good in our own eyes and the eyes of similar people. This is just a mild case of denial. There are many common phrases we use when denying our own imperfections or sinfulness. "They did it too!" "It wasn't me, I didn't do it (when actually we did)." "No harm, no foul." "It's not my fault!" "Well, if they hadn't done what they did, I wouldn't have done what I did!" What are some other ways you see people and institutions denying their shortcoming and brokenness?
2. We can say that we don't care if we are sinful. We can

thumb our noses at God, and anyone else whom we harm, and continue to live how we want to live no matter what. Have you ever heard any of these statements? "I don't care what you think, or if I did hurt you or your feelings." "Get over it." "Quit whining." "Put your big boy pants on." "I am who I am; take me or leave me." "If you can't run with the big dogs, then stay on the porch." "It's a dog eat dog world." What are some other statements that you have heard that are examples of people who don't care how their actions affect others? What are some situations you have experienced where people have responded by not caring about how their actions and attitude affect other people?

3. We can try to cancel out our sin with good deeds. If we do enough good deeds in the world, we can cancel out our evil deeds. Can you do enough good deeds to cancel out your bad deeds? But what happens when there doesn't seem to be any good choice? What happens when it seems like the only thing you could do in a situation is something bad? Does the end justify the means? When we are in charge of making ourselves righteous, we become self-righteous. If we can make ourselves worthy of salvation then we do not need God. Making ourselves righteous seems like an impossible task, and one that will leave us focusing more on ourselves than the Creator of the Universe.
4. We can confess to being sinners and trust in God's mercy.

These options for dealing with our sinfulness have been around for many years.

Discussion Question:
- What are other ways of dealing with our situation as sinners in a sinful world?

In his version of the Gospel, Luke included one example of how two people dealt with their situation as guilty sinners. How we approach someone or a situation makes a difference. In the scripture passage that we are about to read today, we hear the words of two criminals who were crucified with Christ. Have someone from the class read Luke 23:32-43 aloud to the class.

Crucifixion was capital punishment in the time of the Roman Empire. Anyone who was crucified had probably done something really bad in the eyes of the state, something that meant that the person did not deserve to live. Crucifixion was

Notes:

Notes:

meant to be extremely brutal as an example and deterrent against similar crimes. According to the gospels of Matthew, Mark, and Luke, two other people were crucified at the same time and place Jesus was crucified. The writer of the Gospel of Luke called these two men criminals and included some of the words that the two men spoke.

The first criminal "hurled insults" at Jesus saying, "Aren't you the Messiah? Save yourself and us!" (v. 39). Have three different people read the words of the first criminal found in verse 39b of the 23rd chapter of the Gospel of Luke. Each person who reads these words aloud is to read them in an insulting way that is different from the other two readers. However, the second criminal responds in a very different way, and he even seems to scold the first criminal for his irreverent words. Have three different people read the words of the second criminal as found in verses 40-42 of Luke 23. Have each person read the words of the second criminal in three different ways of rebuking him (i.e. rebuking as your father would, as your mother would, as a friend would, as a sibling would, as a teacher would, as an enemy would, etc.).

Discussion Questions:
- How do those different readings of the criminal's words influence how you interpret what they said?
- How would you react to each criminal had you been Jesus?
- How do you feel about the words of each man?
- How did Jesus react to each man?
- Why do you think Jesus responded to each man differently?
- What experiences in your life does this story about Jesus bring to your mind?
- How have you responded to someone who has "hurled insults" or hurt you?
- How does someone's attitude, or the way that someone approaches you, affect how you respond to them?
- How does your attitude, or the way that you approach God, affect how God responds to you?
- What other scripture passages or stories from the Bible does this story bring to your mind?
- This conversation between these three men hanging on crosses was not included in any of the other three Gospels. Why do you think the writer of the Gospel of Luke included this conversation?

How does God respond to sin?

One of the criminals approached God by asking Jesus to remember him when Jesus came into his kingdom (v. 42). Jesus responded to that person's plea for mercy with a promise, "Truly I tell you, today you will be with me in paradise!" (v. 43). In the scripture passages that we read earlier in the lesson, we read how God responds to sin. Refresh your memory with what was promised in each passage: Psalm 14:2-3; Psalm 32:1-5; Psalm 130; Isaiah 6:1-7; Romans 3:21-26; Ephesians 2:1-10; and 1 John 1:8-10.

Discussion Questions:
- How does scripture describe God's response to sin?
- What other scripture passages do these passages bring to your mind?

When we accept God's forgiveness for ourselves, we acknowledge that we are sinful rather than living in a state of denial. When we accept God's forgiveness for ourselves, we acknowledge that we cannot heal ourselves or make things right without God's help. When we accept God's forgiveness for ourselves, we put our faith in God that our relationship has been restored with our Creator and we can begin to work on our relationships with other people.

Live It (5 min.)

Giving Our Sins to God

This is an activity where the teacher and students have a chance to write something sinful they have done, or some part of them that is coming between them and God. Give each person a piece of paper and a pencil. Ask them to write what has come between them and God—some aspect of their life they wish to confess and surrender to God.

Reassure the students no one will read their papers and they won't have to share what they write with the class. Give everyone in the room time to finish what they want to write. After they have finished writing, lead the class in a prayer asking God to forgive us of our sins and to help us to walk in

Notes:

Notes:

God's ways. God knows what is on our minds and will heal our broken hearts.

According to Paul, God knows what we want and need far more than ourselves and the Holy Spirit is actively petitioning God on our behalf. Tell the students that they can deposit the piece of paper in the trash can by the door as they leave the class. They can leave that sin and its burden behind as they begin life as a new creation. The pieces of paper will not be read by anyone. They will be destroyed promptly after church today. Some of them may not be ready to let go of that piece of paper. Do not force or coerce them to leave the paper. Some of them may need to talk and pray with someone before they can let go of that piece of paper.

Encourage anyone who needs to, or wants to, talk with someone about what they wrote to go to their pastor, an elder of the church, a Sunday school teacher, or someone whom they trust and who is strong in their faith in God.

Say: Take a moment to look over the list of "Attitudes" that we made earlier during our class. Pick one that stands out to you.

For our closing prayer, I will begin the prayer by saying, "O Lord, we are..." Then we will go around the room and each one of us will say which ever attitude that stands out to us. It is OK if more than one person says the same attitude. After each person says an attitude, we will all say, "Jesus, remember us when you come into your kingdom."

© 2014 Discipleship Ministry Team of the Ministry Council of the Cumberland Presbyterian Church. All Rights Reserved.

DIGGING DEEPER

The following question is the first question asked to people joining a Cumberland Presbyterian Church as found in the "Directory of Worship" found in the Confession of Faith of the Cumberland Presbyterian Church:

> "Do you repent of your sin and believe Jesus Christ to be your Savior and the Lord of your life?"

The following questions are the questions that are to be asked to someone who is being baptized as outlined in the Book of Common Worship. This book was prepared by the Cumberland Presbyterian Church and the Presbyterian Church (PCUSA).

> Trusting in the gracious mercy of God, do you turn from the ways of sin and renounce evil and its power in the world?
>
> Do you turn to Jesus Christ and accept him as your Lord and Savior, trusting in his grace and love?
>
> Will you be Christ's faithful disciple, obeying his Word and showing his love?

What do we as Cumberland Presbyterians say that we believe about sin?
2.04 As did Adam and Eve, all persons rebel against God, lose the right relationship to God, and become slaves to sin and death. This condition becomes the source of all sinful attitudes and actions.
2.05 In willfully sinning all people become guilty before God and are under divine wrath and judgment, unless saved by God's grace through Jesus Christ.
2.06 The alienation of persons from God affects the rest of creation, so that the whole creation stands in need of God's redemption.

How do we deal with sin?
The four options listed below are examples of how some people have chosen to deal with our sinfulness:
1. We can deny our sinfulness.
2. We can say that we don't care if we are sinful.
3. We can try to cancel out our sin with good deeds.
4. We can confess to being sinners and trust in God's mercy.

These options for dealing with our sinfulness have been around for many years. What are other ways of dealing with our situation as sinners in a sinful world?

What does the Bible say about sin?
Look up the following scripture passages and discuss how humans are described in them: Psalm 14:2-3; Psalm 32:1-5; Psalm 130; Isaiah 6:1-7; Romans 3:21-26; Ephesians 2:1-10; and 1 John 1:8-10.

Do Not Write
by Jeff Ingram

Scripture: John 19:21-22

Theme: We all face rejection— even Jesus. Is that such a bad thing?

Resource List

- Jia Jiang's TEDxAustin Talk: "Surprising Lessons from 100 Days of Rejection" Paper
- Pens
- Newsprint for posting questions
- Markers
- Video capability (laptop, projector, DVD player, speakers, etc.)

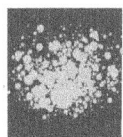

Leader Prep

- Watch Jia Jiang's "Surprising Lessons from 100 Days of Rejection" TED talk.
- Reflect on your own rejections in daily life. It can be found (https://www.youtube.com/watch?v=ZFWyseydTkQ).
- Read John 18 and 19. This will help contextualize the rejection of Jesus throughout his trial and crucifixion.

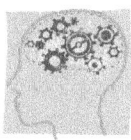

Leader Insight

Connecting to Your Students
Your students face rejection all the time. They place themselves at the world's mercy every day. They go to school every day in an environment where they can be rejected for many reasons. They try out for plays, sports teams, and school projects. They balance time, relationships, and pressure from others. These can be successes or a steady stream of rejection. This can be hard to deal with as a youth.

We all have to deal with the pressures of daily life and those around us. This lesson addresses the potential rejection we all

Notes:

face everyday, while offering encouragement and hope through the story of Jesus' crucifixion.

Explaining the Bible
"Do not write 'The King of the Jews', but that this man claimed to be king of the Jews." That is pretty harsh. These were the words the priests spoke after Pilate had written "King of the Jews" on the cross that Jesus was crucified on. While it's debatable what the reality of the situation was politically, according to Pilate, Jesus' claims of kingship weren't serious. But by beating him, placing him in a purple robe, placing a crown of thorns on his head, and presenting him to the Jewish authorities, Pilate mocked Jesus. (Feasting 307) Jesus was mocked, betrayed, and denied by his closest followers and the Jewish people. He was accused of claiming to be the Son of God.

Jesus never made directly the claim that he was the King of the Jews, only that he was here to serve a greater purpose. His kingdom was "not from this world." (John 18:36) Jesus was arrested because he defied the religious leaders and people claimed him as a king. This claim was seen as an affront to the Emperor of Rome. Claiming to be a king was a crime against Caesar. The crowd says this during the questioning of Jesus and Pilate's questioning of the Jews before Jesus was turned over to the crowd. Jesus was a political threat. The inscription is not made to honor Jesus, but rather to mock and ridicule him and the Jewish people. This is your king? Look at his power compared to that of Caesar.

Theological Underpinnings
Being rejected by the people that he was sent to save was a part of the prophecy that Jesus was fulfilling. He knew throughout his trial and crucifixion that he would be rejected and denied. Jesus neither lashed out, nor was angry.   Jesus even asked for forgiveness for the people that crucified him, even though he was rejected by them.

In this lesson, we will look at the rejection Jesus faced. We will then learn the story of a man named Jia Jang. In his quest to follow his dream, he opened himself up to rejection. As the lesson closes, we will explore what it means for us to open ourselves up to face rejection.

Applying the Lesson to Your Own Life
Rejection. We've all experienced it. We've been rejected by our friends, our co-workers, even random people. It always hurts, whether it is getting rejected in a personal relationship

or for that job promotion we thought we were going to get. Sometimes the only solace we have in rejection is that we know that others are rejected. We know that Jesus was rejected, several times, by several people. Peter denied knowing Jesus. Judas turned Jesus over to the authorities. The crowd rejected and mocked Jesus in his final moments. Then there is this rejection by the priests. This is a slightly more subtle rejection, but definitely one of the more hurtful rejections that Jesus faced. Pilate had them write "The King of the Jews" above Jesus on the cross. The priest rejected Jesus by telling Pilate to change this to "This man said 'I am the King of the Jews."

Jesus knew that he would be rejected. He knew that people would not want him to make claims, be bold, and teach the things he taught. He did it anyway, without fear of rejection from the people he would encounter. Through his courage in life, he was not swayed by the rejection of others.

When have you been rejected? As a teenager, an adult, as a Christian?

When have you rejected others?

We all face rejection. Use this opportunity to connect with your students and their rejection.

If it's not too painful, consider opening up about your own rejection and how you deal/have dealt with it.

Notes:

Notes:

The Lesson

Get Started (15 min.)

Gather your group and begin by having them write answers to these posted prompts:
- Name a time when you were rejected.
- How do you deal with rejection?
- Describe a time you rejected someone.
- How did rejecting someone make you feel?

Allow 10 minutes for everyone to write responses to the posted prompts.

After everyone has had an opportunity to write responses, spend 5 minutes picking out some of the things that were mentioned for each question.

Listen Up (25 min.)

Have someone read John 19:21-22.

Before discussing the passage, show the Jia Jiang video "Surprising Lessons from 100 Days of Rejection." (Approx. 13 min.)

In this video, Jia Jang describes why he embarked on this adventure of being rejected for 100 days. He makes crazy requests of people and expects to get rejected every time. He describes his experience as, "Before Donuts and After Donuts." The ultimate point of Jia's talk is that we have a fear of rejection; Jesus didn't fear rejection. He could have easily shied away from God's purpose in his life and just played it safe, but he didn't. He knew that rejection was coming, but he still continued to do what he was doing.

Discussion Questions:
- What do you think of the challenge that Jia made for himself?
- What were some of the surprising things that happened to Jia?
- Would you be able to do something like this? Why or why Not?

Now What? (10 min.)

Jia says in his talk that "If I open up myself to the world, the world will open up itself to me." This simple statement says a lot about not only what Jia has been doing in the name of improving himself, but what Jesus did when he was preaching.

He opened himself up to the world, and the world rejected him at first. But then people accepted him, just as we have. Spend a few minutes discussing the statement that Jia made towards the end of his talk, and focus on this one point:

Discussion Question:
- How can you open yourself up to the world?

List these ideas on newsprint or a dry erase board. Leave these as a reminder of how we can be open to each other and for the sake of the kingdom.

Notes:

Notes:

Live It (5 min.)

Gather everyone in a circle. In the circle, ask the group to state, or restate, how they will open themselves up to the world in the coming week.

After everyone has had a chance to make their statement, close with a prayer centering on having no more fear of rejection.

Optional: Rejection Therapy

Jia talks about the game, "Rejection Therapy" as his inspiration for his 100 days of rejection. Rules and suggestions for the game can be found here: http://rejectiontherapy.com/ If it is right for your group, put together a Rejection Therapy game. Remember that the key to this is not the rejection itself, but the opening up of yourself to do what you're called to do regardless of fear of rejection

Consider using it as a group activity, rather than as an individual practice.

© 2014 Discipleship Ministry Team of the Ministry Council of the Cumberland Presbyterian Church. All Rights Reserved.

It Is Finished
by Derek Jacks

Scripture: John 19:30

Theme: The central message of the Bible is the redemption of human beings for the glory of God; this is fully accomplished in Jesus' death on the cross in reconciling human beings to God the Father.

Resource List

- A Cross
- Communion elements: juice and bread
- Sermon clip from Billy Graham
- Video capability (laptop, projector, DVD player, speakers, etc.)

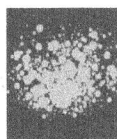

Leader Prep

- The week prior to the lesson, ask your students what the symbol of the cross means to them. The cross is one of the most popular symbols in our world today. Ask your students what immediately comes to their mind when they see a cross. Bring a cross with you to class; you may also encourage your students to bring a cross to class with them (optional).
- Download Billy Graham video from following link (2 minutes): https://www.youtube.com/watch?v=pp-6RoVKTOs
- This lesson will provide a great opportunity for your group to celebrate the Lord's Supper together. If you are not an ordained minister in the Cumberland Presbyterian Church, you will need to have an ordained minister in the Cumberland Presbyterian Church come to the end of your youth meeting to bless the elements, OR you should have an ordained minister consecrate (bless) the bread and the juice prior to the lesson.

Notes:

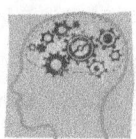

Leader Insight

Connecting to Your Students
What is the significance of Jesus' death on the cross for the world today? How does his death transform our lives? If someone were to ask you or your students, "Why was the cross necessary?" how would you respond? What was finished when Jesus uttered these last words in John's gospel? This lesson will seek to answer these questions from a biblical perspective, along with encouraging your students to have a cross-centered worldview today. The symbol of the cross today is worn often, even by non-believers who don't consider the weight of its message. The cross is more than a fashion statement; for those who have trusted in Christ for the forgiveness of sins, it is the very essence of our lives! When Jesus said, "It is finished," he was saying that sin and death are conquered- the veil of the Temple is torn and we have complete access to God the Father through Christ's atoning sacrifice on the cross (Hebrews 4:14-16). As Paul wrote in 2 Corinthians 5:21, "He (Jesus) who knew no sin became sin, in order that we (human beings) might become the righteousness of God."

Explaining the Bible
John's Gospel is one of the more unique gospels of the four we have in the New Testament (Matthew, Mark, Luke, John). John was considered to be Jesus' closest disciple, and he gives us a beautiful portrait of Jesus throughout his Gospel. One example of this is the "I am" statements. Jesus is the "light of the world"; he is "the way, the truth, and the life"; he is "the good shepherd who lays down his life for his sheep"; he is "the bread of life"; he is the "true vine"; he is "the door"; he is "the resurrection and the life." Each of these statements confirms Jesus' sole authority in salvation. Although there is not a specific "I am" statement in 19:31, Jesus is the one who conquers sin and death by dying for all people. The purpose of John's gospel is clear: that people would believe in the true Son of God, Jesus Christ.

Jesus performs many signs in the Gospel of John. In fact, the only account of Jesus raising Lazarus from the dead is found in John (chapter 11). John also notes at the end of his gospel that there were many signs that Jesus did "in the presence of his disciples," but they could not all be written down. Although the signs Jesus performed were powerful, they were not as powerful as what he would accomplish in his final three words: "It....is...finished." It is here in Jesus' final three words that we see the purpose of God becoming flesh: to save the world (John 3:16). Indeed, no miracle that Jesus performed during his life was as great as the miracle he accomplished by dying on the cross so that human beings could have everlasting life.

The Bible portrays the victory of God as something entirely different from the world's understanding of victory. For example, in sports one team tries to overpower its opponent by doing everything it takes to win a game. When God the Father sought to defeat the power of sin in human beings, he did not do it by setting up a kingdom and conquering the world; rather, he did it by sending his one and only Son, and sending him to die as the reconciler for all human beings who are created in the image of God (Genesis 1:26-27).

D.A. Carson affirms this victory in his commentary on John. In our English text, we may think that Jesus' final words have no element of victory whatsoever. In the original language of John, he uses only one word: tetelestai. Carson writes in his commentary:

> "This is no cry of defeat; nor is it merely an announcement of imminent death (though it is not less than that). The verb 'teleo' from which this form derives denotes the carrying out of a task, and in religious contexts bears the overtone of fulfilling one's religious obligations. Accordingly, in the light of the impending cross, Jesus could earlier cry,
> 'I have brought you glory on earth by completing the work you gave me to do (17:4).
> 'Having loved his own who were in the world, he loved them not only to the end but to
> the full extent mandated by his mission. And so, on the brink of death, Jesus cries out,
> 'It is accomplished!'"

Carson helps us understand the significance of these three words. Jesus' ultimate mission while on the earth was to defeat the curse of sin through shedding his blood for mankind on the cross. As the apostle Paul wrote in Galatians 4, when the fullness of time had come, God sent forth his Son!

Theological Underpinnings
In this lesson, we will help students understand:
1. ...the victory of God accomplished in the death

Notes:

of Christ. God delivers his people from sin by becoming human. John wrote in the prologue of his gospel that he beheld Jesus' glory, and that Jesus was full of "grace and truth" (John 1:14). God the Father accomplishes his victory over sin by revealing Jesus as the one full of grace (love and compassion) and truth (the only one who can provide salvation).

2. ...the importance of the doctrine of the love of God. God the Father chose to reveal his perfect love for human beings by pouring out his very own blood on the cross. The love of God the Father saves human beings, adopts human beings into his family, and will glorify human beings in eternity. At the heart of God's love is the cross of Christ; this gives believers a present hope (Romans 5:5) and a future glory (Romans 8:18).

3. ...the importance of the Lord's Supper to the Christian community. The Lord's Supper is a sacrament that has both individual and communal benefits. It is more than a reminder of the forgiveness of sins—God empowers his people in a mysterious way through the sacrament to live a life of holiness and service. He also unites the diverse members of his body when they celebrate together.

Applying the Lesson to Your Own Life

As you prepare this lesson, think about how you have communicated God's love to those around you (family, friends, co-workers, etc.). It is essential that the Church lives out the greatest commandments taught by Jesus: to love God, and to love our neighbor. The cross is the foundation of God's love for the world today. If a believer cannot communicate what Jesus' death on the cross means for his or her life, then he or she will have a difficult time explaining what it means for God to love people. Reflect on the following passages, which deal with the meaning of the cross:

- 1 Corinthians 1:18
- Galatians 6:14
- Philippians 2:1-11; 3:7-11
- Revelation 7:9-14

If you know of a student that doesn't know Jesus, pray that the Spirit of God would use you to lead them to the cross. Listen to the song, "Lead me to the Cross" by Hillsong, and pray that your students would understand how the cross of Christ is their victory over sin and death!

The Lesson

Get Started (10 min.)

What Does this Cross Mean?

As students enter the room, have your cross on a table in the center of the room. If your students have a cross they have brought to class, ask them to keep it near them for the lesson. Open with this prayer:

> *God our Father, we thank you that you have brought us here to hear from you. We thank you that we can approach you with joy and confidence because of the gift of your Son, Jesus. We thank you for the work of your Holy Spirit, and we pray that you speak to us by your Spirit through your word this morning. We thank you for the cross, and we thank you that you have died for us on the cross so that we might have life eternal. Teach us, Oh Lord, how to live in accordance with your Gospel. May we boldly proclaim the message of the cross to a lost and dying world. In Jesus' name, Amen.*

Discuss the Symbol of the Cross

Begin the lesson by opening with the following question:
- What immediately comes to mind when you see a cross?

Encourage the students to discuss where they see symbols of the cross in their world.
- What do you think of people who wear a cross (jewelry, tattoo, clothing, etc.), yet don't live lives that reflect the Christian life?

Notes:

Leader Tip:
Make sure that students don't gossip about their peers, but rather build one another up by discussing how they can bring change by being passionate followers of Jesus (Luke 9:24-27).

Notes:

Notes:

Listen Up (20 min.)

Read John 19:30.

With what has been discussed, ask your students to now explain what Jesus' death on the cross means. Emphasize the words, "It is finished." Explain to your students how Jesus accomplished the victory over sin and death by dying on the cross for us (see "Explaining the Bible" section).

Discussion Questions:
- Reflect on Jesus' final words, "It is finished." What did he mean by this?
- How have you experienced the reality of these words in your life?
- What implication do these words have on your struggle against sin?

Billy Graham Sermon Clip

Say: *While the symbol of the cross may have little significance to many, it is the very foundation of the Christian life. Our Christian roots are rooted in the cross of Christ. The church (believers) cannot know God the Father apart from God the Son and God the Holy Spirit. As Graham notes in the sermon clip, much of John's gospel is devoted to Jesus' death. God has dwelt among us in the person and work of Jesus Christ, and the cross was his plan from the beginning of time.*

Show the Billy Graham sermon clip.

Now What? (20 min.)

Go back to your cross that you had at the beginning of class

Discussion Questions:
- What does the cross means to you after hearing God's word?
- How has the Scripture changed your view of the cross (if it has changed at all)?

Have the students then begin the process of preparing their hearts for the celebration of the Lord's Supper.

Instruct students that we will partake in the Eucharist, Holy Communion. Offer instrumental music to be played during the time. After they have taken of the elements, they will be given time for reflection. Instruct them there is to be no talking during this time.

> **Leader:** *God be with you!*
> **People:** *And also with you.*
>
> **Prayer:** *As we partake of this bread and juice, we honor the Creator and creation.*
>
> *As these elements are blessed, we celebrate the fellowship of Jesus.*
>
> *All are welcome! Amen!*

Read Luke 22:19-20.

As each class member is served the bread, respond: "The body of Christ broken for you."

As each class member is served the juice respond: "The blood of Christ shed for you."

After a period of reflection, close with the following prayer, or pray your own: *The meal has been shared. God; we give thanks for bread; we give thanks for the fruit of the vine; we give you thanks for your wisdom guiding us along our journey. May we share the good news and the feast with others. Amen.*

Notes:

Leader Tip:
This preparation should include prayer and reading of the Scripture. After about 10 minutes of quiet time, regroup your students and allow them a time to share what they have learned from one another's encouragement.

Notes:

Notes:

Live It (5 min.)

Following the celebration of the supper, leave your students with the following benediction:

May you leave this place empowered by the Holy Spirit to trust in Jesus for all things. May you encourage others who are broken by sin, failure, illness, need, or physical ailment. May you trust that the cross of Christ is sufficient for growing in godliness and holiness. May all you come in contact with be shaped by the work of the Holy Spirit in your life, and may they recognize the One who has saved you for his glory alone, Jesus Christ our Lord. Amen.

© 2014 Discipleship Ministry Team of the Ministry Council of the Cumberland Presbyterian Church. All Rights Reserved.

Into Your Hands, I Commit My Spirit
by Andy McClung

Scripture: Luke 23:46

Theme: Jesus chose to be a victor, rather than a victim. So should we.

Resource List

- Photocopy of "Famous Last Words"
- Photocopies of "In The News"
- A hat or bowl
- Bulletin board and lots of pushpins, or wall/whiteboard and masking tape
- Two signs: "Considered Self Victim" and "Accepted Responsibility"
- Adequate space for students to divide into breakout groups
- Marker board or 3 sheets of newsprint, colorful variety of markers

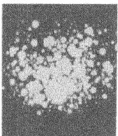

Leader Prep

- Copy and cut "Famous Last Words" in such a way that each quote, and its accompanying explanation, are on a single slip of paper. Fold each of these slips, printing to the inside, and put them all in the hat or bowl.

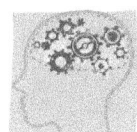

Leader Insight

Connecting to Your Students

A student doing poorly in algebra says the teacher just doesn't like her. A man smokes ten cigarettes a day for thirty years and then blames the tobacco company when he gets cancer. A politician tries to calm citizens' anger over a poor economy by saying he inherited a mess from his predecessor. Two teenage girls blame McDonald's for their obesity. An unproductive employee says his boss unfairly overlooked him for a promotion. A high school dropout complains no one will give her a good-paying job. God asks Adam why he ate the forbidden fruit, and he says Eve gave it to him; she says the serpent tricked her into it.

Notes:

Seeing oneself as a victim may be popular, and teens have plenty of high-profile models for this, but it's a horrible way to live. Jesus, who truly was a victim, refused to consider himself as such.

Explaining the Bible
By combining the four gospel accounts of Jesus' crucifixion, we come up with seven things Jesus said from the cross.

Different scholars, commentators, teachers, and preachers chronologically arrange these seven sayings differently. Some put "It is finished" (John 19:30) as the final one, while some put "Father, into your hands I commit my spirit" (Luke 23:46) as the final one. In Hebrew thinking, seven is the number of completion. That makes Jesus saying, "It is finished/completed" spookily appropriate to be the very last of the seven things Jesus said from the cross. But we don't really know which was said last.

Whether or not "Father, into your hands I commit my spirit" were Jesus' final words, they are significant. They show us that, despite his being targeted by the religious authorities, and despite his being unjustly arrested, and despite his sham of a trial, and despite his being flogged nearly to death, and despite his being beaten and spit upon, and despite his being publicly humiliated, and despite his being nailed to a cross... Jesus had not succumbed to any of this torture.

The Jewish religious leaders, the Roman political leaders, and the Roman executioners/soldiers probably all believed that Jesus' life was in their hands. But they were wrong. Jesus' life was still in his own hands. His life was his to give up, to commit to God.

In John 10:17-18a, Jesus said, "For this reason the Father loves me, because I lay down my life in order to take it up again. No one takes it from me, but I lay it down of my own accord. I have power to lay it down, and I have power to take it up again" (NRSV). In John 10:11 he said, "I am the good shepherd. The good shepherd lays down his life for the sheep" (NRSV). There is no talk here of Jesus's life being taken from him. There is no blaming the Jewish religious leaders, the Roman political leaders, the crowds of Jewish citizens who called for his crucifixion, or even the Roman executioners/soldiers who actually did the deed. Jesus made a conscious decision to lay down his life. Nobody took it from him. It was his choice, his gift to the world.

In other words, Jesus refused to consider himself a victim. Instead, he was a victor over the adversity others put upon him, his own sinful desires, and death itself. When we use Jesus as our model for living, we too can be victors rather than victims.

Persons tend to die as they lived. There's an old story about a man who worked hard all his life to establish many restaurants all over the U.S. whose final words from his deathbed were, "Slice the ham thin." Back in the days when most people died at home rather than in a hospital, a woman known to be incredibly frugal was on her deathbed. She overheard someone in the kitchen preparing to put the kettle on to make some tea and called out, "Use the small eye," meaning the small eye of the stove which used less energy than the larger eye. P.T. Barnum grew up quite poor, but developed into a crafty businessman who continually came up with new ways to earn the public's entertainment dollars. Supposedly, just moments from his death, he inquired about ticket sales that night at his circus in Madison Square Garden. Military men often die on the battlefield. Career criminals often die at the hands of other criminals or in the process of committing a crime. Attention-craving celebrities often die in attention-getting ways such as car crashes, drug overdoses, or suicide. Loving parents often die surrounded by their children and grandchildren. Persons tend to die as they lived.

It really should be no surprise that in the moments before his death Jesus committed his life to God; that's exactly what he had been doing all his life! He never pursued his own will, but sought to do God's will. His life always was committed to God.

And that is why he had no trouble saying, "Father, into your hands I commit my spirit." That was what he'd been doing every minute of every day his entire life. That also should be what every Christian does every minute of every day after accepting Christ as Lord and Savior.

Theological Underpinnings

The Book of Common Worship ("common" means something a group of people do together or "in common," not "ordinary"), produced jointly by the Presbyterian Church (USA) and our own denomination, includes an order of worship to be used at a committal, or graveside, funeral service.

The person officiating says, "In sure and certain hope of the resurrection to eternal life, through our Lord Jesus Christ, we

Notes:

Notes:

commend to almighty God our brother/sister [name], and we commit his/her body to the ground, earth to earth, ashes to ashes, dust to dust."

We "commit" the body to the ground by burying it, certain that one day it will be resurrected. We also "commend" the deceased person to God; we deliver them into God's care with confidence. We don't "commit" a person to God because that's a decision everyone has to make for him or herself— even those raised in church. According to Cumberland Presbyterian theology and polity, children of believers are part of the "household of faith," but it's not until those children profess faith in Jesus Christ for themselves that they are truly Christian. They're not officially members of the congregation until they profess faith and answer the questions for church membership (Confession 4.10, Constitution 2.11, 2.13, 4.10). Children can't rely on their parents' faith forever; they have to take the step to commit themselves to God through Christ.

A distinctive trait of Cumberland Presbyterian theology is that we believe that God gives us the faith to make that choice, to commit ourselves to God through Christ. It's still 100% up to each person whether or not to make that choice, but we're only able to make it because God gives us the faith to do so (Confession of Faith 2.01, 4.01, 4.03, 4.08, 4.10).

Applying the Lesson to Your Own Life
Do you tend to place blame for your own mistakes on someone else, or inanimate objects, or bad luck, or forces beyond your control, or on something else? Or do you readily own up to your mistakes? How do you feel about yourself when you place blame on others? How do you feel when you accept responsibility for your actions and choices?

Do you think too many people refuse to accept responsibility for their own actions? Do think too many people see themselves as victims? Why or why not? Do you see yourself as a victim? If so, how much do you allow that perception to affect your daily life? Your spiritual life?

Consider including the phrase, "God, into your hands I commit my spirit" in your regular prayer time in the coming weeks. Note in your journal how it makes you feel to say those words, and what effect this regular reminder has on your spiritual life.

The Lesson

Get Started (10 min.)

Discussion Question:
- Without saying any names, can you think of somebody who always acts like a victim? Nothing is ever their fault. Somebody has always done something wrong to them. The world owes them something. Life is never fair for them. Do you know anybody who thinks of themselves like that? [Allow only simple yes/no responses.]

Say: *Many people are indeed victimized by others, and we should have compassion for true victims. But right now we're talking about people who try to get out of accepting responsibility for their actions by playing the victim.*

Leaving a few feet between them, tack to the bulletin board, or tape to the wall, the two signs: "Considered Self Victim" and "Accepted Responsibility."

Explain that you have assembled a collection of quotes that are the last words (or in some cases the almost-last words) of various persons who were accused of something, found guilty, and executed for it.

Then ask students to, one-by-one, come to the front of the room and do the following:
1. Take a slip of paper from the hat or bowl
2. Read aloud what's written there
3. Decide if the person mentioned a) died considering himself or herself a victim or b) died accepting responsibility for their actions and choices.
4. Tack or tape the slip of paper below the appropriate sign.

Occasionally, but not every time, ask the class if they agree with the quote's placement. Allow brief discussion or debate. Allow students to change where they place their quotes based on this discussion.

If you have a large class, some students may not get a turn. If you have a small class, everyone will get multiple turns.

Make sure the quote from Jesus (Luke 23:46) is the final slip

Notes:

Leader Tip:
Although some quotes do seem to fit better in one of the categories, there are no real right or wrong answers in this exercise. It's not about giving the right answers, but instead thinking about one's attitudes while facing certain death.

Notes:

taken. Keep it out of the bowl until the bowl is empty and then drop it in, or keep your fingers over the piece of paper until the final student reaches into the bowl. The sneakier you can be about doing this, the greater the effect will be.

Presumably, the final student will have trouble placing the Jesus quote. After all, Jesus had nothing to accept responsibility for, but neither did he consider himself a victim.

Use this hesitation by saying something like: Hmmm… Jesus doesn't really fit into either one of those categories does he? I mean, he had nothing to accept responsibility for, but he didn't consider himself a victim either.

If the student doesn't hesitate and definitively places the Jesus quote, question that choice using words similar to those above, and/or ask the rest of the class if they agree.

Discussion Question:
- Was Jesus a victim? Who victimized him? Did he act like a victim or a victor?

Listen Up (20 min.)

Hang three sheets of newsprint, or divide your white board into three equal sections. Write on the three sheets/areas: Words, Doing, With You.

Tell the students to write what they would want their last words to be (regardless of how they were dying) on the sheet/area labeled Words.

On the Doing section, have them write what they would like to be doing when they die.

On the With You sheet, have them write who they want to be with when they die.

When every student has written on each sheet, read aloud Luke 23:46: Jesus called out with a loud voice, "Father, into your hands I commit my spirit." When he had said this, he breathed his last. (NIV)

Say: *These may have been Jesus' last words. If not, they were close to his last words.*

Discussion Question:
- How do these last words compare to the last words you wrote?

Offer very little comment. If students' "last words" were self-serving or vindictive, or completely unspiritual, it will be obvious; allow students to recognize this on their own.

At some point, explain that "Into your hands I commit my spirit" is part of Psalm 31:5, and is the typical Jewish bedtime prayer— much like our "Now I lay me down to sleep…"

Discussion Question:
- Does knowing this make these words of Jesus any more, or any less, significant? Why/why not?

You might want to point out that by saying these words, Jesus was indicating his complete trust in God. You might also point out that Jesus added "Father" to that ancient prayer, making it far more personal.

Read aloud Luke 23:46.
> Jesus called out with a loud voice, "Father, into your hands I commit my spirit." When he had said this, he breathed his last. (NIV)

Explain that when Jesus died, he was doing pretty much what he had always done: helping others, trusting God, and setting an example for us to follow. Throughout the gospels we see him helping people who are sick, possessed, despised, leading sinful lives, or otherwise separated from society and/or God. Here on the cross he is helping every human being – past, present, and future – by offering a way to escape the consequences of sin. Here at the end of his earthly life, he is trusting God to take care of him. And in all this he is showing us how to "walk through the valley of the shadow of death."

Discussion Question:
- Compare what Jesus was doing when he died to what you said you would want to be doing when you die.

Leader Tip:

It may be confusing to talk about Jesus talking to and trusting in God when we know Jesus was God. This difficulty is part of the mystery of God; our limited human understanding and imagination simply can't fully grasp it.

Notes:

Again, allow discussion, but try to let the students recognize on their own that selfish or pleasure-oriented actions pale in comparison to a self-sacrificing act. You might point out what Jesus was not doing: whining about being a victim or plotting vengeance against his tormentors. Instead, he was trusting God.

Read aloud Luke 23:46.
> Jesus called out with a loud voice, "Father, into your hands I commit my spirit." When he had said this, he breathed his last. (NIV)

Discussion Question:
- So who was with Jesus when he died?

"Mary", "John", "soldiers", and "the two criminals" are all correct answers, but what you're looking for here is "God." Remember, for the first time in his life, Jesus may have felt completely separated from God for a bit while he was on the cross. That may be why he said, "Why have you forsaken me?" But here, just before the end of his earthly life, the intimacy between Jesus and God is fully restored. That intimacy allowed Jesus to face death with assurance. Intimacy with God, available only through Jesus, can allow us to face every scary thing – including, but not limited to, death – with assurance.

Now What? (15 min.)

Divide the class into groups of no more than five students each, even if it means only having two groups. If you have three or fewer students, just do this exercise as a whole class.

Give each group the handout "In the News". Tell them to read either one of the stories and then, as a group, answer the questions on the handout. One student should record the group's answers and be prepared to report those responses to the whole class.

After about five minutes, tell the small groups to do the same with the other story.

After another five minutes, call all groups together. Ask the recorder for each group to summarize the group's responses to the questions. If there is time remaining after all groups have reported, allow feedback, responses, and questions between the groups.

 ## Live It (5 min.)

Say: *Evil people in this world, our own sinful natures, and the devil all try to make us their victims. There's only one way we can be victors rather than victims of these forces: by committing ourselves to God through Jesus Christ.*

Close the class with a prayer thanking God for Jesus and asking God – when he knows it's the right time – to move in the hearts of any who have not yet accepted Jesus Christ as Lord and Savior.

Resources used: anglicanhistory.org, barnum-museum.org, blacksportsonline.com, Book of Common Worship, clark-prosecutor.org, deathcamps.info, fox10tv.com, historylearningsite.co.uk, historywithatwist.wordpress.com, ibtimes.com, murderpedia.org, nydailynews.com, Our Country by Benson Lossing, philosopedia.org, Seven Simple Sermons on the Saviour's Last words by Herschel Ford.
have each person pray for, and with, one of their peers.

Resources: http://www.thesource4ym.com/games/default.aspx?Search=Anywhere

© 2014 Discipleship Ministry Team of the Ministry Council of the Cumberland Presbyterian Church. All Rights Reserved.

FAMOUS LAST (or almost last) WORDS

After apologizing to his family and telling them that he loved them: "The rest of you can kiss my [bleep]."
- James Allen Red Dog, 1993, executed for convicted kidnapping, rape, and murder

"I pray you bear me witness that I met my fate like a brave man."
-John Andre, 1780, executed as a spy

"Well, gentlemen, you are about to see a baked Appel."
-George Appel, 1928, executed by electrocution for killing a police officer

"I'd rather be fishing."
-Jimmy Glass, 1987, executed for murder

"Hurrah for anarchy! This is the happiest moment of my life."
-George Engle, 1886, hanged for a political bombing that killed 11 people

"I'm sorry from the bottom of my heart. I want to thank all of my family and friends who supported and believed in me. I will now spend all of my holidays with my Lord and Savior, Jesus Christ. Peace be with you all. Amen."
-Kenneth Biros, 2009, executed for murder

"How about this for a headline for tomorrow's paper: French Fries."
-James French, 1966, executed by electrocution for murder

"Take a step forward lads – it'll be easier that way."
-Robert Erskine Childers, 1922, executed by firing squad for supporting Ireland as a free state

"Capital punishment: them without the capital get the punishment."
- John Arthur Spenkelink, 1979, executed for murder

"I didn't murder the Hodges family. I've never murdered anybody. I'm going to my death with a clear conscience. "
- Earl Bramblett, 2003, executed for multiple murders

"God bless everybody. Continue to walk with God. Go Cowboys!"
-Jesse Joe Hernandez, 2012, executed for murder

FAMOUS LAST (or almost last) WORDS

"I did not get my Spaghetti-O's. I got spaghetti. I want the press to know this."
-Thomas Grasso, 1995, executed for murdering an 87 year old woman for $12

"There is nothing proper about what you are doing, soldier. But do try to kill me properly."
-Cicero to his assassin, 43 B.C., assassinated for political reasons

"I am guilty. My sentence is just. I deserve my fate. And may God have mercy on my soul."
-William Corder, 1828, executed for murder

After having converted to Catholicism in prison: "I ask God to accept me with mercy."
-Hans Frank, 1946, executed for mass murders in Nazi death camps

"I go from a corruptible, to an incorruptible Crown; where no disturbance can be, no disturbance in the World."
-King Charles I of England, 1649, executed for treason

"I only regret that I have but one life to lose for my country."
-Nathan Hale, 1776, hanged as a spy

"Long live freedom!"
-Hans Scholl, 1943, executed for defying Hitler

"They're not shooting me for deserting the United States Army. They just need to make an example of somebody, and I'm it because I'm an ex-con."
-Eddie Slovik, 1945, executed for desertion

"I'd just like to say I'm sailing with the Rock and I'll be back like Independence Day with Jesus, June 6, like the movie, big mothership and all. I'll be back."
-Aileen Wuornos, 1992, executed for multiple murders

"Tell the governor he just lost my vote. Y'all hurry this along. I'm dying to get out of here."
-Christopher Scott Emmett, 2008, executed for robbery and murder of a co-worker

"Father, into your hands I commit my spirit."
-Jesus, circa A.D. 33, executed by crucifixion for telling the truth (FOR ALLEGEDLY LEADING A REVOLT AGAINST ROME?) THAT'S WHAT HE WAS KILLED FOR LEGALLY

IN THE NEWS
Story #1

A CUSTOMER shopping in a Family Dollar store in Mobile, Alabama, in late 2013, noticed an armed robber leading one of the employees to the front of the store. The customer, legally armed with a handgun, moved closer and heard the robber demand money. Then he saw the robber holding a gun to the kneeling employee's head. The customer drew his handgun and said, "Hey! Don't move." The robber turned toward the customer and the customer fired. "I didn't want to shoot him, but when I saw him swing around so fast I didn't want to get shot either," said the customer.

The robber, Adric White, survived and was taken to the hospital under police custody. As it turns out, he had been arrested a month earlier for another armed robbery and was out on bail.

White's family quickly lodged complaints against the customer and the police, saying that White should not have been shot. A relative said, speaking of the customer who shot White, "If his life was not in danger, if no one had a gun up to him, if no one pointed a gun at him – what gives him the right to think that it's okay to just shoot someone? You should have just left the store and went wherever you had to go in your car or whatever." Family members also said White isn't a bad person but had recently fallen in with bad crowd.

Take a moment to think back on what you've discussed in class today about choosing not to feel like a victim, taking responsibility for your own actions, and making a commitment to God through Jesus.

Now, in your small group, decide what you would say to Adric White's family. Summarize your responses here –

Now, in your small group, decide what you think Jesus would say to Adric White's family. Summarize your responses here –

IN THE NEWS
Story #2

RICHIE PARKER is a well-respected engineer – a chassis and body component designer, to be specific – at Hendrick Motorsports. Richie has ben with Hendrick for eight years. Hendrick is the company behind one of the most successful teams in NASCAR history. Current and past drivers include Jeff Gordon, Jimmie Johnson, Dale Earnhardt, Jr., Kyle Busch, and Darrell Waltrip.

Richie rode a bike when he was a kid. He learned to drive as a teen and now owns his dream car: a restored and customized 1964 Chevy Impala. He graduated from Clemson in 2009.

Richie, however, was born without arms. His father built a bike that allowed him to steer using his chin. Richie himself designed the modifications to his Impala that allow him to steer with his feet. At Hendrick Motorsports, he uses his toes to type on a keyboard and use a mouse. He does not use prosthetic arms or hands. When Richie needs to do something he figures out a way to do it, even if that means designing and building something to allow him to do it.

At his birth, Richie's parents decided not to use his disability as an excuse for why he cannot do things, but rather as a challenge to figure out different ways for him to do everything he could. Richie says that "No" has never been an option in his life; the only question he asks is "How?"

Take a moment to think back on what you've discussed in class today about choosing not to feel like a victim, taking responsibility for your own actions, and making a commitment to God through Jesus.

Now, in your small group, decide what you would say to Richie Parker. Summarize your responses here –

Now, in your small group, decide what you think Jesus would say to Richie Parker. Summarize your responses here –

Truly this was the son of God
by Samantha Hassell

Scripture: Matthew 27:45-54, Mark 15:33-39, John 8:31-32

Theme: The power in the truth of who Jesus is, sets us free. When we recognize and live in that truth, we are changed.

Resource List

- Truth/poop sticks
- 8 ½ x 11 sheets of paper
- Writing utensils
- Scripture questions posted

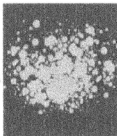

Leader Prep

- Be familiar with the scripture texts and this lesson
- Gather all the necessary supplies.
- Create truth/poop sticks; to make the truth/poop sticks, use a dowel rod, or even popsicle sticks, and attach two pieces of paper to make a hand held sign. On one side write "truth"; on the other write "poop."
- On a sheet of newsprint, or on a marker board, write the scripture questions listed in the "Hear" section of this lesson so the groups can easily see the questions as they work.

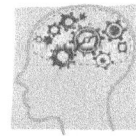

Leader Insight

Connecting to Your Students
"Truth" can be a relative term. For example: "Pizza is delicious," is true for me, but it may not be true for you. "Running 5 miles is a fun way to spend the morning," may be true for me, but it may not be true for you.

And "truth" can be an absolute term. For example, "What goes up, must come down because of gravity," is an absolute truth. Christians believe "Jesus is the Son of God," to be an absolute truth. It could even be argued that there are only a

Notes:

few absolute truths.

Young people are hit with all sorts of "truths." As the adults who love them and get to journey with them, our goal is to help them sort through all of the "truths" they're confronted with, while helping them establish truths for themselves which will guide them as disciples of Christ.

Explaining the Lesson
All three of the synoptic gospels (Matthew, Mark, and Luke) include some words from the Centurion at the cross. The theme of Luke's gospel varies and focuses on the innocence of Jesus in his death; therefore in Luke's account, the Centurion claims, "Certainly this man was innocent," (Luke 23:47). In Matthew and Mark's accounts, however, the Centurion makes a Christological (the nature of the person of Jesus) statement claiming, "Truly this man was God's Son!" For the purposes of this lesson, we will focus on the gospel according to both Matthew and Mark. It's interesting to note how each gospel writer brings the Centurion to this belief. According to Matthew, Jesus' death had cosmic significance: the earth shook, the rocks were split, tombs were open, and many dead were raised and walked about. So upon seeing the earthquake and what took place at the time of Jesus' death, the Centurion came to the belief that Jesus was the Son of God. Mark's account is a little more mysterious. In Mark's gospel, the Centurion makes the same claim, but he makes this based on Jesus' final moments on the cross: "When the centurion, who stood facing him, saw that in this way he breathed his last," he made the claim that Jesus was the Son of God. It leaves me wondering, "What did the centurion see!?" In Jesus' last breath, what was it that brought the centurion to the knowledge that Jesus is the Son of God?

It's okay that Matthew and Mark give different details – the conclusion is the same. I've heard it best explained in this way: each Gospel writer was a painter painting a portrait of the same story. If they each took a photograph, each would be identical. Rather, they each paint the story, which means that some pieces of the painting are left to interpretation and will vary. Ultimately though, they tell the same story – just in different ways. That Matthew and Mark offer varying details doesn't change the fact that the centurion came to an understanding of who Jesus was upon his death.

As a Roman soldier present at Jesus' crucifixion, it's fair to assume that he played an active part in Jesus' death. It's also fair to assume that as a Roman soldier, this man had no belief in Jesus as the Son of God prior to the crucifixion. But when he saw Jesus on the cross, when he witnessed Jesus breathing his last and the events that followed, his eyes were opened to the truth— a truth that he could not deny and which left him proclaiming Jesus as the Son of God. The centurion is a great example of a) the power of truth breaking down barriers b) the importance of being willing to change your mind when it's appropriate and c) being able to let go of what's familiar and cling to a new truth. The centurion went from a soldier doing his job, executing a man accused of treason and blasphemy, to a man who recognized the Christ when he saw him.

Theological Underpinnings
Students will begin with a game that takes a light hearted look at what we think to be true or not. Some truths will be shocking, some gross, some just fun. This activity is meant to get them thinking about what they know, don't know, and maybe don't want to know.

Students will then break into groups to explore the scripture texts. While each group will explore either the Matthew text or the Mark text, they will share their findings with the opposite group.

You will then invite your group to consider what they know to be true and share those absolute truths with the rest of the group. You will offer a benediction over your young people before you send them out praying that they will know the truth as they seek to be disciples.

Applying the Lesson to Your Own Life
What are your absolute truths?

Make a list of three things that you know without a doubt to be true. Now imagine that one of those truths was challenged. Can you recall a time when a truth you believed in was contradicted, and you began to see things in a new way? How did it affect you?

How about the first time that you really understood who Jesus is and what he reveals about the nature of God? Did your reality, or way of seeing things, change? It can be a relief to see the truth, but it can also be a shock to our system. Thank you for the work you do in revealing the truth of Jesus Christ to your young people. It's an awesome and humbling responsibility.

Leader Tip:
Even if God doesn't directly cause everything to happen, we still should do as 1 Thessalonians 5:18 says, and thank God for all good things.

Notes:

The Lesson

Get Started (15 min.)

Begin with this game, adapted from www.thesource4ym.com called "Truth or Poop."

Divide into 2 teams. Have 1 contestant come up for each team for each question. Give them the "truth/poop" signs that you made before class. They will hear a fact being read that may or may not be true. If they think it's true, they hold up the "truth" side of the sign. If they believe it's not true, they hold up the "poop" side of the sign. For each correct answer they win points for their team. The team with the most points at the end wins the game.

100 Points
1. Steve Jobs was 15 when he co-founded Apple Computers, Inc. POOP: He was 21.
2. Fish scales can be found in many lipsticks. TRUTH
3. Foot rot disease in sheep can be found in the horns as well as the feet. POOP: Only the feet get foot rot.
4. By law, women's underwear cannot be hung outdoors during autumn or winter in Los Angeles. TRUTH
5. Coca-cola would be green if color weren't added to it. TRUTH

200 Points
1. Texas eats more Spam than any other U.S. state. POOP: Hawaii does.
2. The most popular sport among college women in the U.S. is volleyball. POOP: It is basketball.
3. Before anyone may step inside the Oval Office, they must salute the American flag. POOP: This is not required.
4. The collective noun for a group of whales is a "watch." POOP: The group is called a "pod."
5. It's against the law to burp in a church in Nebraska. TRUTH

300 Points
1. When the moon blocks the path of the sun, it is called a lunar eclipse. POOP: A lunar eclipse occurs when the earth interrupts sunlight shining on the moon.
2. The family name of the kangaroo, Macropodidae,

means "big foot." TRUTH
3. A ziggurat is a species of rat native to South America. POOP: It's a Babylonian pyramid.
4. The second state to join the union was Massachusetts. POOP: It was Pennsylvania.
5. One quarter of the bones in your body are in your feet. TRUTH
6. Jesus is the son of God TRUTH

After the game, tally up the score and celebrate everyone's brilliance.

Discussion Questions:
- Were you especially surprised by any of the statements?
- What is it like to realize that something is true that you never knew to be true before?
- Invite participants to share an experience where they learned something to be true after not previously knowing or believing it.

Listen Up (20 min.)

Divide students into two groups: a "Matthew" group and a "Mark" group.

Give each group paper (newsprint, notebooks, it doesn't matter) and writing utensils.

Have the following questions posted in the room, and ask small groups to read their passage together and record their answers on the paper provided:
- According to your passage, it was dark between what hours?
- What did Jesus cry out at about 3:00?
- Who did people believe Jesus was calling out to?
- What did they offer him?
- After Jesus was offered the sponge, what did he do?
- What are all the things that happened after Jesus breathed his last?
- What did the Centurion say?
- What made the Centurion say what he said?

Leader Tip:
It will help the discussion if you will share your own example. It doesn't have to be anything life shattering (it can be, but doesn't have to be). Be willing to give your own example.

Leader Tip:
Groups can be as small as 2 people or as large as 5-6. If your group is larger than a dozen, it would be appropriate to have 2 "Matthew" groups or 2 "Mark" groups.

Leader Tip:
Most of their answers will be the same. The pieces that differ are what happened after Jesus breathed his last and what caused the Centurion to proclaim Jesus as the Son of God.

Give students plenty of time to work (7-8 minutes should be plenty). Call groups back together, and invite the Matthew group to read their text aloud to the Mark group. As they're reading, ask the Mark group to listen and watch their notes for anything that is different. Ask them just to jot down the differences, but refrain from commenting.

Next, invite the Mark group to do the same: to read their text aloud to the Matthew group while the Matthew groups listens for, and makes notes of, any differences without commenting just yet.

Discussion Questions:
- What were the differences?
- What were the similarities?
- Why do you think there were pieces of the story that varied?
- Does this make a difference to the truth of the story?

*Use some of the info from the "Explaining the Bible" section in order to help students understand that the details may vary, but the point of the story remains. Let this lead you into discussion on the Centurion's role in Jesus' crucifixion.

- The Centurion's claim that Jesus is the Son of God was so significant that three of the four gospel writers include it in their version of the story – why?

Now What? (15 min.)

This activity is meant to be a contemplative prayer activity. Invite students to spend some time thinking about what they know to be true about Jesus (and God). Invite them to spend some time making a list of those truths. You should make your own list too. Feel free to play some music quietly in the background while this is going on. After a few minutes, invite the students to share their lists. Be willing to share yours.

Assure students that there are no right or wrong lists. Assure students that it's okay if there is only one thing on their list that they know to be truth. Assure them that it's okay to have questions and doubts – the centurion certainly had doubts but when confronted with the truth, he saw it for what it was.

 ## Live It (5 min.)

Gather in a circle and offer the following benediction over your students: *John 8:31 begins, 'Jesus said to the Jews,' but let's read it this way: Jesus said to the teenagers circled up in their youth room, 'If you continue in my word, you are truly my disciples; and you will know the truth, and the truth will make you free.' My prayer for each of you is that you will know the truth as you seek to be Jesus' followers.*

© 2014 Discipleship Ministry Team of the Ministry Council of the Cumberland Presbyterian Church. All Rights Reserved.

Notes:

About the contributors...

Christopher Anderson is the father of two boys who keep him busy. Jake is thirteen and Caleb is twelve. He loves to watch them play sports but, most importantly, loves watching them grow as they learn the teachings of Jesus Christ to serve others. Christopher is a Cumberland Presbyterian minister and missionary from Batesville, Arkansas. He is completing his Master of Divinity degree at Memphis Theological Seminary and then intends to pursue a doctorate. He is actively part of a homeless ministry in Memphis that provides food and care for those in need.

Samantha Hassell is a Christian Educator who has been serving the Cumberland Presbyterian Church since 2001, when she graduated from what is now Bethel University. Samantha has served congregations in both Tennessee and Kentucky and has had opportunity to serve on Presbyterial and Denominational boards and teams, as well. When God calls Samantha to do something God does so in a still small voice and, when that doesn't get her attention, with an opportunity dropped in her lap. Writing for **Faith Out Loud** was no different. Although stubborn when God calls, her love for young people and her desire to help them to grow as disciples keeps her answering, "Yes!" Samantha and her husband, Victor, have three children and serve together at Sturgis Cumberland Presbyterian Church in Sturgis, Kentucky.

Jeff Ingram is a lifelong Cumberland Presbyterian and a member of the Cumberland Presbyterian Church of Germantown, Tennessee. Jeff is very active in the Cumberland Presbyterian Church serving as a member of the Young Adult Ministry Council and as special staff for the Cumberland Presbyterian Youth Conference and for Presbyterian Youth Triennium. Professionally, Jeff is a community organizer and specialized in translating online activity into offline action. Jeff works with Worship Times, a web development company specializing in web design for churches and other ministries. Jeff holds a Bachelors degree in Anthropology from Middle Tennessee State University and a masters degree in political science from the University of Memphis.

Rev. Derek Jacks has served as the pastor of Homewood Cumberland Presbyterian Church in Birmingham, Alabama, for four years. Prior to his time at HCPC, he served nine years as youth pastor of Rocky Ridge Cumberland Presbyterian Church and he currently directs Grace Presbytery's annual Winter Youth Convocation in Gatlinburg, Tennessee. Derek has been married to his lovely wife Cindy for twelve years and they have three children; Ava, Braden, and Drew.

Rev. Dr. Andy McClung has been teaching Cumberland Presbyterian youth and adults since 1988, both in person and through his writing. A double graduate of Memphis Theological Seminary (M.Div., 1994 and D.Min., 2002), Andy has served congregations in Alabama, Arkansas, Mississippi, and Tennessee. Cursed with a dry sense of humor and blessed with a love for the Cumberland Presbyterian Church, he lives in Memphis and continues to teach, preach, write, and serve the church at the presbyterial, synodic, and denominational levels.

Rev. Jennifer Newell is the Senior Pastor at First Cumberland in downtown Cleveland, Tennessee. Jennifer is a graduate of University Tennessee Chattanooga and the PAS Program. She and her husband Chuck are parents to three youth of their own: Ellie, Evan, and Zoe. The Newells enjoy working impossibly-hard jigsaw puzzles, eating good barbecue, and fighting their cats for control of the house.

Rev. Mark Rackley is the pastor of the Bartow Cumberland Presbyterian Church. Mark has served the Bartow CPC since 1998. He earned a B.S. in mathematics from Bethel University and an M.Div. from Union Theological Seminary in Richmond, Virginia, and a M.A. in Christian Education from the Presbyterian School of Christian Education where he met his wife Michelle. Michelle and Mark have been married since 1994. They now have three children: Sarah, Paul, and Anna.

Series editor for *Faith Out Loud* is Susan Guin Groce. Line editor is Mark A. Taylor. Electronic processing and incidental layout by Matthew H. Gore. *Faith Out Loud* logo and cover design are by Joanna Bellis. Produced for the Discipleship Ministry Team of the Ministry Council of the Cumberland Presbyterian Church.

www.ingramcontent.com/pod-product-compliance
Lightning Source LLC
Chambersburg PA
CBHW080541300426
44111CB00017B/2821